Hiring the Best

How to Staff Your Department Right the First Time

Hiring the Best

How to Staff Your Department Right the First Time

Martin Yate

BOB ADAMS, INC.
PUBLISHERS
Holbrook, Massachusetts

Also by Martin Yate:

Keeping the Best . . . and Other Thoughts on Building a Super Competitive Workforce

Knock 'em Dead With Great Answers to Tough Interview Questions

Resumes that Knock 'em Dead

The above titles are available at your local bookstore. If you cannot find them at your local bookstore, you may order them by contacting the publisher at 1-800-872-5627 (617/767-8100 in Massachusetts). Please check your local bookstore first.

Published by
Bob Adams, Inc.
260 Center Street
Holbrook, Massachusetts 02343

ISBN: 1-55850-873-2
ISBN: 1-55850-872-4 (paperback)

Manufactured in the United States of America

A B C D E F G H I J
A B C D E F G H I J (paperback)

Every effort has been made to provide accurate and nondiscriminatory information in this book, but it is not intended to be a legal resource. As with all issues concerning the hiring and/or dismissal of employees, consult an attorney if you have any doubts about the legitimacy or legal ramifications of the use of a question or technique in this book in your company, industry, or state. The publisher assumes no liability for damages direct or incidental related to the individual hiring or dismissal decisions of any reader of this book.

—The Publisher

This publication is designed to provide accurate and authoritative information with regard to the subject matter covered. It is sold with the understanding that the publisher is not engaged in rendering legal, accounting, or other professional advice. If legal advice or other expert assistance is required, the services of a competent professional person should be sought.

—From a Declaration of Principles *jointly adopted by a Committee of the American Bar Association and a Committee of Publishers and Associations*

For information about our audio products, write us at:
Newbridge Book Clubs, 3000 Cindel Drive, Delran, NJ 08370

Cover design by Joyce Weston

Acknowledgments

My thanks to the following: For believing that we could produce a truly different and vital management book, my editor Eric Blume and my publisher Bob Adams; for ongoing support in many different ways, my friends at the Dunhill Personnel System around the country—especially Stan Hart, President of Dunhill of Troy and the Michigan Association of Personnel Consultants, and Mike Badgett, president of Dunhill of Cherry Hills Village (Colorado) and treasurer of the Colorado Association of Personnel Consultants; for their special attention and efforts, Adia Personnel Services, Management Recruiters, and Sales Recruiters International; for their assistance on the new chapters for this, the second edition of the book, Marilyn Huzar of Career Services Chicago, Dr. Maxwell Keck of John Carroll University, Lou Scott and Alan Schoenberg of MRI, and author Judy Schockert of NJIT; and finally, my thanks to all those people who offered help, insight, and contacts in the world of corporate America.

Dedication:

To Jill, to say the least

Contents

Four: The Cracks in the Resume 61

What is the worth of a resume? The four resume styles and what they are designed to do. Exaggerations of modest truths. On getting snowed by action verbs. Educational claims, and the difference between credentials and accomplishments. The Personalized Matching Sheet. Using the resume to formulate your knock-out questions.

Five: From Phoner to Short List 71

Saving time, money, frustration, and embarrassment with telephone interviews. Cutting the applicant list, streamlining the interview process. Seventeen phoner questions to ask the applicant. What to do with the people you can't use, the people you're not sure about. The ground rules for those you want to see.

Six: The Art and Science of Interviewing 83

The Art of the Question: Twelve basic techniques designed to get facts, no fluff. The Art of the Conversation: The six ploys for forwarding the conversation and gaining the most information. The Science of Interviewing Styles: The four basic tacks to take, their strengths, their weaknesses. The all-embracing approach: Judging Ability, Willingness, and Manageability. Planning the interview's structure. Initial preparations.

Seven: Ability 105

Is the candidate able to do the job? Over 50 questions that probe basic responsibilities, communications skills, ability to work with all levels and make decisions, reasons for leaving jobs, worker/manager relationships. What your aim is with each question, and what danger signs to be alert for.

One: You, Your Staff, Your Career

A myth in corporate America is ruining careers and profits—who knows which is worse? The myth is that upon promotion into management, you become mystically endowed with all the skills necessary to manage and to create a team that gets the job done. That is a manager's job, after all: To get work done through others. It means picking them right in the first place, because it is impossible to *manage* effectively without *hiring* effectively. So you, the manager, are ultimately responsible for the effectiveness of your team. That should be common knowledge; so should the fact that those managers who do not hire the right people therefore cannot manage appropriately, and ultimately get the axe.

No one knows how many managers have stalled their careers through an inability to make the right hires. We have all heard about someone who is a great engineer (or accountant or salesman) with great top-office potential, but who turns out to be a lousy manager. Often though, such an evaluation could be proved wrong on closer examination. The manager's problem is often little more than being unable to *interview* effectively. It is a dirty secret for many, and a sad comment on old-style management practices, that managers are not usually taught this key managerial art. It is something we feel we are expected to know, or that comes with experience. Couple that feeling with the average ego and you get,

"It's easy enough to interview; I know a good one when I see one; it's sort of a gut feeling."

Today, many managers are struggling to come to terms with the final costs of self-deception, *before it is too late.*

A company's personnel is its heart, though traditional accounting methodologies have consistently denied the workforce an assessable value. A company may have the best plant and equipment available, but how much knowledge and dedication, how many skills and personalities does a company need to survive and prosper? It is the *people* who make or break an organization, who produce and ship the product, who perform the service. To talk of the body corporate is to talk of its lifeblood, the workers, those who are managed, coursing through the halls. Your workforce is priceless.

Yet the average manager's life is a running battle, frequently fought with inherited troops and their marginal competency and/or bad attitudes. Few ever ask or are given the opportunity to clean house, and less than two in ten are ever encouraged to attend a seminar or read a book about prudent hiring practices. The end result? We staff and maintain our companies as amateurs. Now is that any way for professionals to behave?

A labor department study shows that 50% of new hires last only six months in their new jobs. Can you believe it? Now common sense tells you that some of these hires were superstars and were rapidly promoted; a good portion of the others either quit or were fired. That's the good news: At least decisions were made in all these instances. What about the rest, the great mass of clock-watchers who just scrape by over the years, missing deadlines, being out sick, spreading discontent, coming in two hours late in the morning and then leaving two hours early to make up for it. To paraphrase Gilbert and Sullivan, "A manager's lot is not an 'appy one."

Bad hires affect the company, the individual, and you—though not necessarily in that order. The wrong person doing the wrong job is harmful to the body corporate's health. Many wrong people multiply this malady, and then you have a debilitating disease. Now, as business believes very strongly in a surgical approach to medicine, if the disease is localized in *your* department, it could ruin your entire day—or your entire career.

We have all made bad hires and worse excuses: "I dunno, boss, I learned him and I learned him, and I bought him books but all he's done is eat the pages." Yet in all cases, the cause of the bad hire can be traced to one of the following reasons:

- Poor analysis of job functions
- Poor analysis of necessary personality-skill profile.
- Inadequate initial screening
- Inadequate *interviewing* techniques
- Inadequate *questioning* techniques
- Poor utilization of "second opinions"
- Company and career/money expectations were over- or inappropriately sold
- References were not checked.

In short, the manager failed to ask either himself or the interviewee the right questions at the right time; and perhaps even failed to interpret the answers given to his questions adequately.

Hiring the Best is a revolutionary new approach to hiring the right people. You get a practical approach to interviewing that can be read tonight and used tomorrow. You will discover how to see beneath the surface of those shiny resumes and discover what they are trying to hide from you. You will learn how and when to use a telephone as a screening device and specifically what questions to ask. And for the face-to-face interviews and multiple interviews, you'll find over four hundred specific questions to ask and what the candidates' answers will reveal about themselves.

But more than showing you how to hire the right person today, *Hiring the Best* synthesizes all the most effective interviewing techniques currently available, so that you will never get fooled again by the apparently perfect applicant.

Today there are a handful of fashionable interviewing styles: Situational, Personality Profile, Stress, and Behavioral, to name the four best. Proponents of each claim theirs to be the only way to the truth behind the candidate's interview facade. They are wrong. Each style has both strengths and weaknesses. But take the best of each, fuse the result with common sense, add the sophisticated probing techniques of investigative journalists and headhunters, and you will have the single most powerful and practical employee selection system in existence.

This system will assure that you get answers to the three most important questions that guarantee a good hire:

1. Able to do the job. Often the hiring decision is on ability alone. While important, here it is merely the first step in ensuring consistently successful hires.

2. Willing to do the job. There can be a distinct gap between ability and willingness to do the job. Take salespeople as an example: The high turnover in this field has led to accusations of lack of professionalism in some quarters. This lack is merely the symptom of a hiring problem. Many salespeople are hired because they appear to have the ability to do the job; all too frequently this can mean a glib tongue. A glib tongue, however, does not always guarantee the enormous self-confidence and determination necessary for success in this field. How many of us could take the awful knocks that are part and parcel of, say, sales and still keep our self-esteem intact? Here lies the problem: A certain salesman wants the opportunity and seems to be a good bet, but how do you find out whether he has the *willingness* to take the rough with the smooth that his—and every—job demands? Determining willingness is the second evaluative approach this book will teach you.

3. Manageable once on the job. The third level of a candidate's evaluation, of paramount importance to a successful hire, is the determination of manageability of each potential employee. A person able and willing, but nontheless unmanageable, is not for you. If you don't relish the idea of catering to a spoiled brat, determining manageability will help you find employees who act their age, not their shoe size. With over two hundred questions covering these three areas, you will see right into a candidate's soul. You will go beyond the tired old excuses of the unconsciously incompetent interviewer who claims, "I'll know him when I see him."

The interview is a measured and ritualistic mating dance—and you have the choice of partners. It should have all the appearances of a relaxed conversation and produce as much information as an F.B.I. dossier. Seems like a tall order? Not when you have studied *Hiring the Best.*

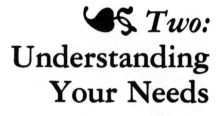

Two: Understanding Your Needs

"Always give your department a directional check-up before starting a hiring cycle," states Charles Gray, president of Dunhill Personnel System. "It's a golden opportunity to improve the caliber of your organization."

Such an opportunity can be disguised in many ways. For example, business is good, and a staff increase is called for; or someone finally gave you a good reason to fire him or her; or maybe someone quit for pastures new. Whatever the reason, you can either fill the slot and repeat past mistakes, or learn from them and create a winning department.

Using the same job description, the same hiring process you've always used, and the same few interview questions, usually means that you will give birth to the same old problems down the road. To avoid this, give your department that all-important once-over and ask yourself some questions before you do anything: Is the department living up to your expectations? has the company made any recent directional changes that should change the manpower make-up of your team? do you really need another engineer or account executive? could you perhaps save money and increase output to the desired level by providing the group with another top-notch administrative assistant? do you really want to hire three junior salespeople just because that's what the budget calls for? will you consider recruiting a heavyweight from the competition, someone who has already made his or her mistakes elsewhere?

The alternative to asking yourself these questions is to be reactive, to charge ahead, as so many do, and adjust needs and job descriptions after a few interviews. You'll find, however, that if you don't know what body or bodies you're looking for, the chances will be that you won't recognize the right one when you see it. Your career deserves better.

Perhaps you are worried that making changes will upset existing staff. If so, remember that the manager who lets employees dictate their job functions is a manager who will soon be looking for another job.

If your company has written job descriptions, don't trust them: They are too vague for your needs. You can easily generate your own as part of your informal directional check-up. Here's how:

Have your staff develop their own job descriptions. You will notice when reviewing the paperwork where the strengths and weaknesses and even gaps are in the department. Look carefully for the cracks and ask yourself what type of person will fill them and strengthen the team.

List the five major functional responsibilities of the vacant position, those areas in which the employee will be spending the majority of time every day. Check the relative importance of each one; don't over-emphasize minor duties involved in each. Then, list the critical skills or special knowledge for each function that a person must possess to perform it.

Remember, though, that the person you hire won't be the picture of perfection; no one is. In the early days of their success, the Marx Brothers went to Chasen's restaurant in Los Angeles. Harpo, who *did* speak in real life, looked down the long French menu and said, "Yes, please, and a cup of coffee." The moral is: Don't be greedy. Go through your functional demands and separate the "must-haves" from the "nice-to-haves." You can't have it all, and long-lived managers know that water-walkers are hard to find and difficult to handle. Opt for good swimmers every time. As you develop these "must-haves" and "nice-to haves," consider the position's level of interaction with other people or departments and any special skills this requires.

Understanding Your Needs

Find out what educational background is necessary to do the job and what educational background is desirable. Be sure that you differentiate between the two. Unless you intend to verify that degree (and have done so historically) don't put too much store by it. The chances could be as high as three in ten that it isn't what it appears to be. Relying on a degree as a basis for hiring or not hiring is, in most cases, a habit now functionally moribund. Use educational background as a signpost of determination and an ability to learn. Then, use the questioning techniques in *Hiring the Best* to make sure you don't rely too heavily on academic criteria for your ultimate decision-making.

Know what depth of experience you need. This is another important and confusing area. Give yourself a range, but be prepared to look at promising people from outside that range. A sharp youngster with four years of progressively diverse experience could often be a better bet than the ten-year seasoned pro, who has in reality repeated one year of experience ten times.

If you are looking for a promotion, you must give consideration to succession planning. You cannot move up without finding a replacement, so you may want to hire strength. Therefore, don't rule out truly seasoned professionals: They made their costly mistakes on someone else's payroll and because they know what they want out of life, are less likely to use you to get ahead. The extra money such a person can cost you will usually be worth the investment.

Create realistic expectations about that intangible area covering experience, education, and job stability. If you are looking for someone with an Ivy League education and twelve years on the same job, you might end up with someone with rich parents and who is afraid of change. On the other hand, a recent Korn Ferry study showed that the typical senior executive did have 17 years on that particular job. There are two sides to most arguments, so just be sure you don't argue yourself into a practically indefensible position.

Hiring the Best

Finally, to get the right person, consider whether you should lower your sights, raise the salary, change the title or take other actions to make the job more attractive to potential employees.

Defining the "ability" aspects of the job is a major step. However, there is a world of difference between "can-do" and "will-do." (If this is a difficult distinction for you, let me introduce you to my two-year-old son, who is a living embodiment of the difference!) Words like "character" and "behavior" and "personality" are important here. They can all be confusing, especially in business, where for many years such words have come to mean an upright moral character and the demeanor of a gentleman or lady. The difficulty comes when we try to use such loose definitions of these words to help us hire effectively. Different jobs require different personality types.

Listed below, there are some 17 key personality traits, in three profile categories, that should be considered and evaluated by the prudent manager during an interview. Any or all could be important for the job that you are trying to fill. Check to see which traits are important to you. The traits you require can affect the questions you plan to ask, and the meaning of the answers you subsequently hear.

Personal Profile:

These traits can reveal basic character, a personal portrait that can broadly affect various aspects of any job.

Drive: Has a desire to get things done; is goal- rather than task-oriented; has an ability to make decisions and to avoid busy work; breaks overwhelming tasks into their component parts.

Motivation: Looks for new challenges; has enthusiasm and a willingness to ask questions; can motivate others through their own interest in doing a good job.

Communication: Can talk and write to people at all levels (which, in our information age, is increasingly important).

Chemistry: Does not get rattled and point the finger of blame; wears a smile; has confidence without self-importance; is cooperative with others; demonstrates leadership by an ability to draw a team together.
Energy: Always gives that extra effort in the small things as well as the important matters.
Determination: Does not back off when the going gets tough; has the ability to cope; can be assertive when necessary; is, at the same time, shrewd enough to know when it is time to back off.
Confidence: Has no braggadocio; is poised, friendly, honest with all employees, high and low; yet knows when to keep a secret.

Professional Profile:

These professional traits can reveal loyalty to a cause, person or company, and speak well of a person's reliability and trustworthiness.

Reliability: Follows up on self; does not rely on others to ensure that a job is well done; keeps management informed.
Integrity: Takes responsibility for own actions, whether good or bad; makes decisions in the best interests of the company, not on whim or personal preference.
Dedication: Has a commitment to tasks and projects; does whatever is necessary to see a project through to completion on deadline. (This is the subtle difference between dedication and determination—from the personal profile—that will temper the possibilities of bullheadedness.)
Pride: Has pride in trade or profession; takes the extra step and always pays attention to details to see the job is done to the best of ability.
Analytical Skills: Weighs the pros and cons; does not jump at the first solution that presents itself; analyzes the short-and long-term benefits of a solution against all its possible negatives; possesses the perception and insight that leads to good judgment.
Listening Skills: Listens and understands rather than waits for a chance to speak; has attentiveness that complements analytical skills.

Business Profile:

These are the characteristics that show a person understands that you are in business to make a profit.

Efficiency: Always keeps an eye open for wastages of time, effort, resources, and money.
Economy: Knows the difference between expensive and cheap solutions to problems; spends your money as if it were his or her own.
Procedures: Knows that procedures usually exist for good reason, and won't work around them; has a willingness to keep you informed; follows the chain of command (meaning that you get to know what's going on in the department before *your* boss does); does not implement own "improved" procedures or organize others to do so.
Profit: Knows it's the reason we are all here.

In deciding which of these traits are important to you, don't be like Harpo. Some you gotta have, others would just be nice.

Now you know what it takes to do the job, both in skills and the personality traits that spell willingness. The next step is finding applicants, right?

Three: Recruitment in the '90s

The '90s, I predict, will come to be known both as the Worker Bust Era and the Decade of Full Employment. Everyone who wants a job will have one; unfortunately, the ones you want won't necessarily want the jobs you have to offer, and the ones you get won't necessarily have the skills you need.

Today, every potential member of the work force that will be in place in the year 2000 has already been born (in fact, this group is now in grade school).

The projected worker shortages at the entry level will bring private sector employers, the military, and other institutions into greater and greater competition. The labor shortage will affect both the quality and quantity of the workers in our organizations, and employers will have to pay higher entry level wages to attract skilled workers. (They will also have to devote more resources and time to training and developing less skilled workers with an eye toward placing them in more demanding positions.) Organizations that want the most productive employees must change their thinking about recruitment and about what, exactly, constitutes that elusive concept we call "corporate fit."

Special Considerations

A little demographic background is probably in order here with regard to women and minorities in the labor market.

Women first entered the work force in significant numbers during the Industrial Revolution. Prior to that, women who worked outside the home were usually engaged in menial or domestic work. The demands of the period encompassing the two world wars led to a further expansion of the number of women in the work force, but these were primarily young and single women who returned to their traditional role of mother and homemaker when they married.

Things could hardly be more different as we enter the final decade of the twentieth century. Women workers today tend to stay in the work force over the long term, and this pattern is expected to remain in force for the foreseeable future. The April 1988 *Training and Development Journal* (the nation's leading forum for the discussion of human resources issues) notes that women are now the majority in university and college freshman classes, and that women account for one-third of the enrollment in law, medicine, and business schools. These trends are supported by Department of Labor statistics that indicate that 1992 will see women comprising over 60% of the work force.

The number of two-income couples will continue to increase, and these couples will, increasingly, decide to raise families. This will lead to scheduling problems as partners try to balance their personal and professional lives. We must bear in mind, through all of this, that the working mother can no longer be expected to tolerate being relegated to the status of an uneducated peon working for the minimum wage. As we have seen, women at all levels are going to constitute the mainstay of our work force.

Even if, historically, women have dropped out of the labor market upon reaching childbearing age, we must now accept that we are faced with a different set of women—and a different set of principles by which they can be expected to live their lives. Sixty percent of mothers of school-age children are working, an increase of one quarter over the 1970 rate. The figures for mothers of pre-school children show a similarly dramatic increase. Don't imagine for a moment that these women are working for what used to be called "pin money." They are working out of economic necessity.

The changes facing corporate America are no less stark when we turn to the role of minority workers in the labor pool. By the year 2000, it is estimated that 20% of our work force will be made up of native non-white workers (that number escalates sharply, of course, when non-white immigrant workers are included). This means that there is more at stake than simple corporate altruism when organizations fail to recruit minorities, women, single parents, and the physically challenged. It is a matter, not of fashionable community relations work, but rather of survival, to reach out to these new workers; companies that do not heed the demographic writing on the wall will only place themselves at a significant competitive disadvantage by striving to remain white and male-dominated.

It is imperative that we not merely mouth acceptance to the new demands made by today's work force, but take specific steps to change the way we do things when it comes to finding good people to fill positions. Unless there is a continual influx of new blood, it is only natural that old methods will persist. The danger is that, in the current environment, our adherence to those old methods of recruitment is just as likely to lead to atrophy and degeneration as that much more feared corporate malady, "losing touch with your customers."

Indeed, a company-wide acceptance of the importance of a diverse, well-trained work force is one of the most elemental preconditions for business success in the coming decade. Financial plans, sales targets, and long-term projections are all moot unless they are anchored in a solid understanding of the labor supply and a knowledge of what it will take to attract good people over time. If you don't have the horses to pull the wagon, it won't matter a whit that you want to go to California; you ain't gonna make it over the trail.

So: how to recruit the best? By speaking to their needs, values, and dreams; by adequately acknowledging their potential for success as well as their qualifications. We must realize that jobs are now going to have to be packaged (like the products they are) if we are to attract our company's most important consumer: the employee.

In the process, we are likely to shift our priorities somewhat, and place less emphasis on hiring the person who can perform 100% of the predetermined parameters of the job. Instead, we must allow ourselves a little more leeway to tailor the job to a person's existing skills, and use any resulting "learning curve" time to provide the challenge and enrichment that will keep the new employee motivated.

To paraphrase Bob Boschert, founder of Silicon Valley's Boschert Associates and one of the forefathers of the "knowledge era," recruitment in the '90s will be a little like running around in front of a steamroller. You can outrun the steamroller easily at any given moment, but if you ever sit down, you are going to get squashed. I offer this analogy as a gentle reminder that there are no recruitment shortcuts in the decade of full employment—only a comprehensive program will put you at a competitive advantage.

People Power

Henry Ford once said that you could repossess all his factories and burn all his warehouses to the ground, but that if you only left him his people he could rebuild everything that had been lost. Mr. Ford was a shrewd judge of character and an acknowledged master at surrounding himself with the very best employees; it is this crucial ability we must try to translate into contemporary terms.

Steve Finkel, a noted recruitment specialist, tells the story of an outfit with an important position to fill. The company advertised in *The Wall Street Journal* with an ad that did not reveal the employer (the job in question was a sensitive and confidential position); the responses, however, left a lot to be desired. Then an eminent retained search firm convinced the company that the "quiet confidence of a retained search" was the route to take. The company was advised that this search for a senior executive would be a difficult one, and would require a $25,000 retainer and six months of down time.

The search firm, true to its word, came back with a recommendation six months later: The company should promote the current assistant to the vacant position into the job.

Paying $25,000 to be told you hired the right person two years ago was an embarrassing lesson, and one that all of corporate America would do well to heed.

All too often we go outside to find that "special someone" who has one key skill we covet, and then cheerfully invest vast amounts of money, time, and effort to bring them up to speed on the other nine critical aspects of the job for which they have no particular aptitude. Usually, when this occurs, there sits in the ranks a proven commodity aching for recognition who already has the nine skills necessary to perform most of the job's duties. What message are we sending to that worker?

With every vacant position that must be filled, look first within your own ranks. It saves time, money, embarrassment and start-up days. It improves morale among current employees. It demonstrates that the company encourages and rewards honest effort and competence.

Modern times demand increased productivity from us all, and the new worker, unlike his generally more docile forbears of twenty or thirty years past, is dissatisfied without meaningful recognition and growth opportunities on the job. Take advantage of this situation by searching within the department to see which team members would welcome and benefit from increased responsibilities. Show yourself to be a manager who helps people grow, and your team will walk over hot coals for you. Show yourself as a more typical manager—the kind who takes credit for all successes, but blames all failures on subordinates—and you will find yourself managing a lot of empty chairs; those potentially loyal employees will up and find themselves a supervisor who *will* champion their cause.

Having looked within your own department, you can, if you feel it is appropriate, canvas colleagues in other areas of the company for suitable candidates. However, as gifts are usually worth what you pay for them, you should be wary of the colleague who offers you his or her "prize employee." You may simply be inheriting someone else's productivity vacuum by taking on such a person.

If searches in both your department and the company at large do not yield the right candidate(s), examine your personal files and company records for suitable candidates. If this involves the human resources department, you can (and should) do more than just put in a formal request.

Hiring the Best

Human resources is perhaps the most notoriously overworked and underdeveloped department of the contemporary American corporation. Its residents deserve your understanding and help. To benefit from their best efforts, do whatever you can to get involved with the search yourself. Make an appearance; let everyone know you're the manager who actually wants to assist in departmental searches, not just another insistent, gray, disembodied voice issuing orders. It's true that this approach may result only in your being presented with a daunting pile of dog-eared resumes, but make the effort to wade through the stack. Your ideal candidate could be hiding somewhere in there.

The next step is to take advantage of the grapevine. Pass the word at your professional associations and clubs, and to friends and business associates: you're looking for a good so-and-so; do they know anyone?

While you can approach this part of the search with optimism, scrutinize closely the recommendations you receive at this stage. Managers often make the mistake of treating such recommendations as endorsements, using the interview only as a confirmation of a decision to hire. Remember that a poor hire will not affect the reputation of the person who passed the name along, but *will* affect the way *you* are perceived. Accept referrals for what they are: suggestions about people who might possibly be worth talking to, nothing more. After all, isn't that what you mean when you give referrals to others?

The grapevine will only solve your problems some of the time. You cannot rely on it as your sole recruitment method.

Advertising: Newspapers

Advertising is simply a way to reach out and make contact with potential employees. For your advertising to be effective, you will have to ensure that your message reaches and has an impact on the correct audience, and this usually takes some effort.

The average Sunday newspaper carries more than a dozen pages of employment-oriented advertising; each of those pages is likely to feature more than a hundred advertisements. Your needs are going to be in competition with the needs of many hundreds of other firms. How will you stand out from the crowd?

The challenge is similar to that faced by the proprietor of a single boutique situated in a suburban mega-mall. While being in the mall in the first place is a sensible marketing decision because of the volume of the foot traffic, the challenge is to find a way to draw both the serious shopper and the casual browser through the door. The savvy retailer realizes that while the serious shopper pays today's bills, today's browser pays tomorrow's bills. Similarly, the highly qualified candidate who contacts you and is in the midst of a serious, systematized job search may be of greatest interest to you now, but the one who is "just looking" at the opportunities you have to offer may also prove valuable to you sometime down the road.

Critics of advertising claim that only the unemployed and employed but terminally dissatisfied read the help wanted pages, and that all the advertiser can expect to hear from are the dregs of the work force. This is not true. Research has proven that while advertising will draw *some* undesirable elements, it is the single most effective way to reach people who are actively engaged in a job search. In a typical week, you can expect to reach over 55% of these people through advertising.

You can also expect to reach around 60% of the hidden labor pool through advertising. The hidden labor pool is made up of those people who are actually fairly happy where they are, but would change jobs for the right opportunity and thus will keep their eyes open. The hidden labor market also includes people who claim absolutely no interest in changing jobs, yet still read the want ads regularly, for reasons that may have to do with monitoring current business trends.

The intelligent advertiser will not only recognize the importance of advertising as a way to reach today's job changer, but also as an effective public relations tool and promotional device to attract tomorrow's job changer (who is equally important).

Grab the Reader's Attention

ACME MANAGAERS
CAN"T TYPE7 FOR BEANs:
WE NEED
EXPERIENCED
WORdProCESSORS—QUIKC!

The first step in getting a response to your advertisement is to get it read. What we read in newspapers depends largely on the headlines: a good grabber will win readers.

I suggest that you follow three headline rules.

- While the headline doesn't have to be witty, it must address your audience.
- The headline must promote qualities that are likely to appeal to the reader.
- The headline must mention the job title.

Remember, too, that headlines are no good if they don't stand out. Use a bold, distinctive type that is attractive and easy to read. Make use of white space so the reader's eyes can focus without strain. Logos or illustrations from a clip art book or disk can also help you grab the audience's attention.

You may be tempted to fill one advertisement with a whole laundry list of openings in an effort to "get your money's worth." The only time this can be justified, however, is when the openings are all related to one another in some obvious way. Jumbling all your openings together in one ad with no regard for whether the ad as a whole is of interest to any given reader is a recipe for wasted space. Virtually no one will read your ad and you will have wasted time, money, and effort.

Almost all classified advertisements are alphabetized; the ad is keyed by its first letter and listed appropriately. This gives one pause when composing a headline; beginning your ad with "word processors" will only leave you to bring up the rear!

There are definite advantages to beginning your headline with a word that begins with "A"—for one thing, it will almost certainly be placed near the beginning of the section and receive wider readership than if it were placed elsewhere. There is also a good argument (for those with budgets that can accommodate a few more ads, anyway) for supplementing your main ad with a small "teaser" ad under, say, "S" for Secretarial and/or "O" for Office Personnel.

> **SECRETARIES: Acme needs word processors. See our ad under "A." 617/555-8354.**

The Message

The headline wins attention, but it is the message in the body copy that encourages the reader to take the next step. And the next step is not to buy a candy bar or spend twenty minutes with an encyclopedia salesman; the next step is to ask for a chance to work with your company, a possibility that could change the reader's whole life. Most of us resist change; it is necessary to give the potential employee a good reason to make the move to your firm.

To write an effective advertisement, you will need all the facts at hand: all the "must-haves" and all the "nice-to-haves" you'd like to see in the applicant, as well as all the pluses about the job and the company.

On a separate sheet of paper, write one to two sentences about each of the following headings.

- Job title
- Type of work
- Major skills required
- Educational requirements
- Career possibilities
- Location
- Company selling points
- Training
- Personal development/career progression

- Equipment
- Environment
- Work conditions
- Salary, benefits, and other incentives

The Job

The description of the job's requirements is of major importance to your readers. The reader wants to know if a good match exists just as much as you do. You need to include information about the responsibilities, of course, but at the same time you should avoid the temptation to get too specific.

By saying something like "CAD/CAM Engineer wanted; must have B.A. and 4 yrs CAD/CAM experience," you may well get some responses if the rest of the ad is attractive. But what do you lose? Just about every engineer with less than four years of CAD/CAM experience will decide not to contact you because of the perceived underqualification. And virtually every engineer with significantly more than that amount of CAD/CAM experience will do the same thing because of the perceived overqualification.

The more "must-haves" you put in an ad, the more potential respondents you will lose. Even the "minimum standard" of a bachelor's degree is somewhat suspect. Why rule out all those competent professionals who might otherwise be acceptable? Why rule out those who are currently engaged in gaining the degree?

Corporate America tends to overemphasize the importance of academic credentials. Unless there is a firm and adhered-to policy of verifying all educational claims on resumes, there is absolutely no point in making a particular level of academic attainment a mandatory requirement for a job. Too many people play fast and loose with the facts.

To find the best employees and have the best human resource pool, cast your net wide and use an exceptionally fine mesh. Make advertisements "specifically vague," and future-oriented as well. The ad must be specific enough to whet the reader's appetite, but vague enough to keep people from ruling themselves out; the ad must be future-oriented, talking about challenges and opportunities rather than those imposing "must-haves." There will be time to separate the winners from the losers later. (And remember: the losers for this particular position may be shoo-ins for next month's openings.)

Look at the body copy of these two ads. As you read them, ask yourself which one is likely to get the most responses and why.

> **INDUSTRIAL ENGINEER with BSIE, minimum seven years' experience. Must have at least five years of experience in production line design. Acme is a $1 billion hardware manufacturer with an 18% growth rate. Promotional opportunities for right candidate.**

> **INDUSTRIAL DESIGNER to accept the challenges of production line design in one of the nation's state-of-the-art manufacturing facilities. Acme is a $1 billion hardware manufacturer with an 18% growth rate. The top professional we select will join a company that traditionally promotes to management from within.**

There's no contest. The second ad is much more appealing, and is likely to generate many more responses than the first. True, some of the responses will be from people who don't have exactly the skill package you need today: they will either be too light or too heavy on experience. But it cannot be over emphasized that today's unsuitable application could be just what you need tomorrow, and with the average fill time for professional positions running between three and six months, building your files could be a real advantage for you later on.

Admittedly, what I'm proposing here entails taking a different approach to advertising, and indeed to recruitment as a whole. But the benefits to this method are well worth the effort and adjustment.

The body copy of the advertisement, then, should address the job in terms of the opportunities it offers. Note the way the second ad phrased this: " . . . to accept the challenges of production line design in one of the nation's state-of-the-art manufacturing facilities."

The ad should talk up the company as a desirable place to work: "Acme is a $1 billion hardware manufacturer with an 18% growth rate. The top professional we select will join a company that traditionally promotes to management from within." Never assume that your company is either a household word or is generally recognized as a great place to work. Instead, consistently use your help-wanted advertisements as public relations vehicles to send the message that your company is progressive, professional, and a terrific place to work.

Money Talks

Whether or not to include salary in the ad is a difficult question. Doing so can be imprudent: If current employees earning considerably less see the ad, you may have trouble in the ranks. In these situations, the position we are trying to fill has, all too often, been vacated by someone who was unhappy and moved on to greener pastures. Whether or not this is the case, though, there is little point in losing the good will of the people you have trained and nurtured by demonstrating that you are prepared to pay more for outsiders.

Remember, too, however, that advertisements that do not include some mention of remuneration get only half the response rate of ads that do. While you can improve the number of inquiries by specifying an exact salary, you can include something like "Salary range starts at $30,000; the right candidate can expect a salary and benefit package commensurate with experience."

Other options would include "Competitive salary," "Salary dependent upon experience," and "Excellent salary for the right candidate." While these are not as effective as mentioning specific dollar ranges, they are infinitely preferable to making no mention whatsoever of money.

Action

Of course, your advertisement can include all the right inducements about the job, money, and firm, and still not get the kind of response you want and deserve. The key remaining variable is how you ask applicants to respond. If your goal is to keep things nice and quiet around the personnel office, use something along these lines: "Send resume with six references to Box 983452."

On the other hand, if you prefer to personalize the proceedings, build interest, and increase responses, there are better approaches to consider. Here's one: "Let's get together. Call Sam Corker at 617/555-3465 to arrange a meeting, or send a resume to Acme at P.O. Box 983452, Ocean Point, New York, 11759."

If you give a telephone number and a name, it is vital that the named individual be consistently available during the ad's pull time, which can extend well beyond the actual day of publication.

Creating Interesting Copy

Whenever possible, use an attractive feature of the job in your headline, then expand on that feature in your body copy.

Cut impotent words and phrases. If you scan the want ads, you'll come across a fair number of ads with phrases like, "Applications are invited for the position of . . .". This is a waste of space, advertising money, and the reader's attention. Of *course* applications are invited for the position in question; why else is someone paying to have a message placed in the classified section? Your advertisements tell potential applicants who you are; avoid saying you are pompous, redundant, and self-important.

Get right into the attractive parts of the job; jump into the body copy with inducements that are specifically vague and future-oriented. Don't be satisfied with a dry, factual recitation of the requirements; turn them into an emotional appeal and highlight the positive features of the opportunity.

Never use gender-specific structure (for instance, "The right applicant will find his salary and benefits package extremely competitive"). Not only is this sexist and illegal, it also turns off precious potential applicants. Better to talk directly to the reader in terms of "you" and all the advantages of the job.

When Should You Advertise?

The answer here is really very simple: Sunday and, perhaps, one other day. There may be one additional day that pulls exceptionally well for help-wanted advertisements in your local metropolitan newspaper. In New York City, for instance, Wednesday is a big day for secretarial advertising.

Tuesday, Wednesday, and Thursday are usually your best candidates for the add-on day. Do a column count of the major newspapers in your area over a period of two weeks; see which days carry the heaviest advertising load.

Beyond the Newspaper

There are some alternatives for print advertising, including pennysavers and association and trade publications.

Pennysavers are the independent classified and help wanted publications that are usually distributed for free in and around major metropolitan areas. They include a significant amount of help-wanted advertising, and can be effective recruitment tools in specific geographic regions if they are used consistently. Few employers, however, have experienced success with sporadic use of these papers.

Association and trade publications can also be effective tools for filling professional positions. Placement on the page is vitally important in these media. Following is a list, in descending order, of the best positions to have in magazines.

- First right hand page
- Back cover
- Inside front cover
- Page facing contents
- Inside rear cover
- Page facing cover article
- Page facing inside rear cover
- Early right hand page
- Early left hand page

Snappy headlines and the greatest copy in the world are of no benefit if your masterpiece goes unseen. The placement of your advertisement, as well as its position on the page, can make all the difference: do not place an ad without having a good idea of where it will run in the publication. (In general, for a newspaper, the rule is to stay as close to the right-hand corner of a page, and as far above the fold, as possible.)

Radio

Radio has proven effective for many companies as a recruitment medium, provided the objective is to fill long-term or multiple openings (as opposed to single vacancies).

Perhaps the most attractive aspect of radio is its ability to help you target your market precisely. A radio station's format is carefully structured to attract a certain type of listener for the specific purpose of selling air time to advertisers. This means that if you wish to reach people over eighteen and younger than twenty-five with at least a high school diploma (or any other similar profile), radio can do it for you.

What's more, because the medium is not yet widely seen as a recruitment vehicle, you can, with good ads, dominate without too much difficulty, thereby attaining what the advertising people refer to as "top of the mind awareness" in your target group. In so doing, you can give your organization's image a real boost.

Radio advertising can be a great recruitment method when you want to call the audience to action; specifically, it is effective if you want to invite people to an open house, to see you at an upcoming job fair, or to direct potential applicants to your advertisement in a newspaper. Bear in mind that radio often catches the listener at a time when jotting down a telephone number is impractical (i.e., during the drive home). You can make your telephone number more memorable by obtaining a vanity number; typically, this costs only around $40 a year. Which is easier to retain: 212/555-5627, or 212/555-JOBS?

Are radio campaigns expensive? They certainly can be. The price per minute may not seem overwhelming, but the problem is that one radio spot is more or less useless. Radio advertising requires constant repetition if it is to be effective. Even considering the costs involved, however, it is a good vehicle for many firms.

The rule of thumb is that a campaign should last a minimum of a week and feature not less than thirty separate spots. The technique is to blitz the audience, rest, then blitz again.

(It is worth noting here in passing that television has yet to prove itself as an effective recruitment medium. It is simply too expensive.)

Job Fairs

Job fairs have been one of the big recruitment successes of the last two decades. These fairs can be set up as a co-operative effort between a group of companies, as a profit-making enterprise by a professional job fair company, or even by the local Chamber of Commerce.

Let's assume that you buy a booth at a fair organized by a private firm that specializes in such gatherings. What are you getting for the $500 to $4000 you will pay? Essentially, you are buying into a giant advertising campaign in the hope that it will draw enough attendees to justify your participation.

Job fairs do a ton of repeat business, which is evidence enough of their success. However, the fact that these fairs are successful for the proprietors does not mean that they are necessarily right for finding the types of people you are looking for at any given time.

It isn't enough to ask the promoter, "Say, do your fairs tend to pull swamp gas reciprocation engineers and and methane throttle specialists?" The answer will invariably be "yes"; the promoter is out to make things look as good as possible to you, and, with two to four thousand people wandering through the door, those types of applicants may occasionally show up at the fair. The question is not whether *any* of the types of applicants you want will attend, but *how many*.

The secret is to look at the types of positions you have recruited for successfully *without* using job fairs. If the task at hand requires you to recruit outside that area, then consider attending a job fair, but make sure it is one where these types of people have been recruited successfully in the past.

It is also advisable to ask the promoter to do something special to help attract the types of people you need. Virtually all job fair companies have developed extensive mailing lists; part of their budget is set aside for direct mail campaigns. You can ask the promoter to insert something for you in the mailings that are sent out to promote the fair.

Bear in mind that while smaller job fair companies may promise you the moon and give every good effort, they often don't have the resources necessary to mount a sustained campaign and build a good following. Established companies, by contrast, will have large client bases, extensive mailing lists, and comparatively deeper pockets (an important consideration, since you are buying into a promotional event). The exception here would be the job fair put on by your local chamber of commerce; these organizations have been known to sponsor high-visibility fairs that are quite cost-effective.

When attending a job fair as an exhibitor, you must present your company attractively, and with exactly as much attention to concerns of buyer perception and public relations as any consumer products or advertising firm. A handmade paper banner and a pile of application forms simply won't do the job; you and your company must be packaged for the event. Make sure that your booth looks top-notch, that the people representing your firm are articulate, polite, and professional, and that potential applicants will not feel put off by overaggressive "hard sell" techniques. (It's worth noting that few if any hires are made at the booth: such hires are not the reason you came to the job fair in the first place. The objective is to generate applications and resumes and follow up on them later.)

Disadvantages to job fairs would include their occasional logistical problems. These fairs can be (and often are) adversely affected by the weather. Even with an indoor facility, attendance may plummet when there is a thunderstorm or snow flurry, and since the advertising is usually geared toward a specific time and place, rain dates, guarantees, and refunds are highly unlikely to be part of the package.

Job fairs, then, can be effective, but even insiders agree that they are not the be-all and end-all recruitment solution some may suggest. They should be considered one part of a balanced recruitment program; used intelligently, they can enhance your company's image and recognition in the marketplace at the same time they are generating resumes. As one participant told me, "The best reason to exhibit at a job fair is not so much to get employees—although it does do that—but rather to get exposure and let the workers in the area know that my company exists and is a good place to work. That way, when they read my ad, or when my recruiter or headhunter calls, they know who we are. We're no longer an unknown quantity."

Employee Referral Programs

It is hard to imagine a better source for referring high quality employees than your current staff. This is not only a good plan for locating strong candidates, but also a wonderful way to show that you appreciate and listen to employees. (It is usually recommended that you put an exclamation point next to the "thank you" by paying a modest bonus to the employee who refers a new hire.) However, the technique can backfire, and a degree of caution is suggested.

There are quite a few horror stories of employees neglecting their normal duties to become full-time recruiters without anyone asking them to do so. In extreme cases, employees may steal referrals from headhunters and offer them as their own, forcing the employer into a difficult position if the ruse is discovered. On occasion, you'll even hear of an employee who, dissatisfied with the referral bonus offered, channels his or her referral on the sly through an unscrupulous headhunter and ignores the employee referral process completely.

Beyond cloak-and-dagger maneuverings such as these, there are some more fundamental problems to consider. One is that birds of a feather really do flock together: machinists don't usually number software designers in their circle of close friends. Confidentiality is another stumbling block. When friends and colleagues are referring one another, keeping sensitive information (such as salary) from becoming widely known becomes even more difficult than usual.

Keeping all the above in mind, you should begin your employee referral program at the beginning and explain the rules of the game to employees in such a way that misperceptions and opportunistic episodes are kept to a minimum. Of course, the employee must feel that there is a tangible benefit to making a referral. Incentives can vary, and may include prizes (a household appliance, for instance, or a paid vacation) and monetary compensation—from a token sum for help in filling a clerical position, up to several thousand dollars for successful referral of a key management employee. (Human resources people and line managers, by the way, are often excluded from these programs to avoid the perception of a conflict of interest.)

A cheap but effective program can be set up using the Grand Prize concept: every time an employee makes a successful referral, a nominal financial reward is given, and the name of the person referring the new employee is entered for a prize drawing. At the end of the program, something of high perceived value, such as a vacation trip to Hawaii, is awarded.

Such programs take time and effort to set up properly; once they are in place, they must be maintained with posters, announcements at meetings, bulletins, and the like.

Other Considerations for the Employee Referral Program

You may wish to stipulate that no referral is considered valid until the new employee has passed the probationary period mandated by your company, and that any moneys or other rewards will be payable only at that time.

Important: With monetary rewards, all parties must recognize that the sums paid will be considered taxable income by the Internal Revenue Service. Employees should be made aware of any deductions well ahead of time, or, if none are made, should be informed that the income is taxable and must be handled accordingly. If these details are ignored, the best-intentioned program in the world can lead to misunderstanding, conflict, and morale problems in the work force.

University Co-op Programs

For the prudent manager eager to enhance company stability over the long term, campus recruitment and organized co-op programs can be extremely attractive alternatives.

Traditionally, co-ops have meant major companies visiting campuses and selecting students to work for them through a semester. This process benefits both parties. The student gets work experience and, eventually, a higher starting salary that reflects that experience. The employer gets the opportunity to hand-pick key future players after having them under close scrutiny for a considerable period.

These days, it is not just the larger companies who stand to benefit from co-op programs; the estimates are that we can expect a shortfall of almost four million entry level workers by 1993. This is a trend with far-reaching implications for even small- and medium-sized firms. Companies of just about every size that wish to have the new recruits they will need to compete in the years ahead must seriously consider getting more heavily involved in campus recruiting.

Fortunately, if you decide to move into this area of recruiting, the colleges and universities will be on your side. Whether the institution in question is a prestigious Ivy League school or a two-year technical college in the heartlands, the administrators will have come to realize that now, more than ever, their ability to place the alumni/ae at the end of their studies will dramatically affect the school's ability to attract students in the first place. You are virtually assured of a warm reception and a helping hand from the schools you approach.

Today, the very nature of co-ops has changed; they can, of course, maintain the standard semester-a-year profile, but it is becoming more common to see work structured around a long vacation or on a part-time basis.

There is certainly nothing to lose by following the co-op path, and there are no minimum requirements you must meet. Even if you need only one or two people a year, virtually any college or university career planning officer will work with you. All it takes is a telephone call; after an initial consultation, referrals can start within a week (but plan on somewhat longer initially until things are running smoothly).

Of course, there are challenges for both sides in this kind of endeavor. Students usually don't want to put off graduation for a year, and companies may experience short-term scheduling and management problems with some of the "rookies." But adjustments can be made, and the potential benefits far outweigh the occasional difficulties.

Beware—there is no point in initiating a co-op program for your company if the participating managers treat the students like slave labor or drones. If this is the prevailing attitude, you will defeat the undertaking's purpose. The recruits will simply reject offers of full-time employment and spread ill will to other students and to the placement office. If, on the other hand, you offer challenging work, equitable pay, and a good measure of professional respect, you will have established firm foundations for an ongoing college recruitment program that will provide your company with the professional and management leadership it will need to succeed in the year 2000 and beyond.

Taking Another Look at the Government as a Recruitment Source

In overlooking state and federal government sources when it comes to recruitment, corporate America has been doing itself a grave injustice. Consider the following true story.

A major computer memory company in Silicon Valley was faced with a problem: serious labor shortfalls in manufacturing. Turnover approached 40%, even though double minimum wage was the starting point for the company's *unskilled* workers, and even though the benefits and surroundings were among the best in the area. Advertising hadn't worked; job fairs (more of a long-term recruitment option, as we've seen) hadn't, either. There wasn't a headhunter to be found who would deign to attempt a search for workers in the categories in question.

What was left to do? The only option left was the state unemployment office, long considered to be the last resting place of the terminally unemployable. In desperation, management made the call and explained the problem in a straightforward way. No one had any right to expect that it would work out as well as it did (thirty-five good hires) or as fast as it did (in a matter of months, the company went from shortfall to waiting-list status), but the company's last resort turned out to be remarkably effective. The state office not only called the company to refer every vaguely suitable candidate, but also recommended the company to all and sundry as a most desirable employer. (The topper is that the firm actually built up tax credits that reached six figures by the end of a twelve-month period!)

Who ended up getting hired? Well, they sure weren't all male Caucasians with a perfect physical profile: management revised its thinking and made an effort to give underemployed sectors of our society a shot. Women, minorities, the physically challenged, and even some of the mentally challenged were all represented, and the results were truly inspiring. These neglected members of the American family have been consistently sold short in the workplace in the past; by working with state officials, the computer company found that, given the opportunity and support, such workers can become a firm's most loyal and motivated employees.

Generating these kinds of results through a partnership with civil servants isn't as difficult as you may think. All that is necessary is an understanding of what *demotivates* government workers, and heading the list is that awful sense of working in a vacuum because all of one's good efforts have always gone and will always go unnoticed. When they are convinced that their work will make a difference to the people they refer and the employers they refer them to, most unemployment office personnel will exhibit the attention, motivation, and persistence we associate with the private sector. (And don't forget that government workers have managers, too; they are usually as eager as the next person to prove how great they are to higher-ups.)

Flex Hours and Job Sharing

Most people, when asked to think of the typical American family, still envision a working father, a mother who is the homemaker, and perhaps two children. In fact, this picture hasn't truly reflected life in America since the middle part of the 1960s; today, only 5% of all American families fit this description.

There is no average household anymore: it is estimated that upwards of 70% of the people entering the work force through the year 2000 will be women and minorities. Many of our workers will provide anything but a "traditional" profile, what with the death of the nuclear family, the increase in single-parent families, and the rise of the two-career couple. Employers must be open to innovation, especially considering that the unemployment rate may continue to hover in the low single digits for the next few years.

Two of the most effective alternative recruitment ideas that have arisen recently are flexible hours and job sharing. It may come as a surprise that the federal government and the healthcare industry—neither considered particularly cutting-edge in nature—have been the real pioneers in these two areas, but such is the case. Approximately 20% of all federal employees take advantage of some form of flexible scheduling; companies in the healthcare field simply couldn't get along without flex time and job sharing. (Consider for a moment the remarkable record of your own local hospital. In all likelihood, it has not shut its doors for a second since the day it opened. For some institutions, this means continuous operation, 24 hours a day and 365 days a year, not merely for decades but for centuries!)

How do the two ideas differ? Flex time is simply the approach of stepping away from the traditional nine-to-five concept in recognition of the increasingly complex time demands of our employees. The idea is often intertwined with that of job sharing, the system whereby people assume joint responsibility for the completion of work normally allotted to one full-time employee.

Permit me to share a story here that illustrates how important these ideas are today. There is a street in San Jose, California known as Stevens Creek Boulevard; it is one of the two or three highest volume areas for automobile sales in the world. As you might expect, competition for good sales reps on this street is fierce. At one dealership worked a single parent—a father—who was the highest producing sales rep in his organization. After his divorce, he had found it literally impossible to get his daughter to daycare and make it to work by 8:30 in the morning. He tried to talk about this problem with his manager, but heard something along the lines of, "Sounds like a personal problem; around here, everyone starts at 8:30. Always have, always will."

The father was left with no choice: he started looking for another job. He contacted the manager of a competitive dealership, who could hardly believe his luck. "It was like manna from heaven," the competing manager remembers. "Here I had the choice of letting one of the best salesmen on the boulevard slip through my fingers, or letting him come in to work fifteen minutes late and make the time up at the end of the shift. It was no contest. He's broken all his previous personal records since coming to work here. I'm convinced the performance I'm getting is the result of our showing just a little decency and concern for him as a person."

Combining flex hours with job sharing gets a little more complex, but at the same time opens up a totally new and untapped labor market.

The key to job sharing is to look at jobs as hours, not as positions. Whereas usually there is one person doing one job forty hours a week, under job sharing there might be two, three, or even four people combining hours to do that same job. The division can be made in whatever way attracts the most and best workers. This approach is beginning to show remarkable results in areas of low unemployment (where, often, the only alternative is to leave the position unfilled).

Job sharing is appropriate for virtually all non-management positions. It is a superior way to attract those who are returning to the work force after (or while) raising a family; many such employees are resuming careers after a marital dislocation. These people represent a major pool of talent that is going largely untapped.

Make no mistake: there is top-notch professional talent to be had within the ranks of the job-sharers, not simply support workers. By 1988, almost 35% of the female MBAs of 1977 had already left the work force. Many of these departed to have children. Increasingly, however, women want to return to the work force after childbirth and regain a productive position in the business community, even if responsibilities to their children (and our new recruits for the year 2000 and beyond) makes returning full-time impractical. Job sharing enables a number of workers (usually two) to team up to make solid, major-league contributions.

Job sharing does carry its own special challenges and problems. For one thing, paper trails become extremely important. (Most teams, however, develop or re-establish the necessary skills quite rapidly.) What's more, the manager may wake up one morning and learn of one team member's departure, which means losing whatever chemistry existed between the two. Fortunately, retention among job-sharing teams is proving to be well above average, and when one person does leave, the remaining team member often becomes a highly motivated recruiter.

Scheduling the teams can be difficult. In effect, the manager must abandon the idea of "having a staff" of ten people beavering away for forty hours a week, and begin thinking instead of being responsible for the management of 400 hours. The adjustment, for most, is well worth the effort, and the end result is more motivated and committed workers.

Employment Services

Corporations choose their lawyers, their accountants, their advertising agencies, and their public relations firms with care and prudence. All of these outside professionals are important to the success of the company. Yet when it comes time to choose an outside employment service—the people who supply the employees that are the lifeblood of the organization—the attitude is often downright cavalier. Why?

There are distinctly different types of employment services; here is the basic breakdown.

- Permanent agencies where the candidate pays the fee.
- Permanent agencies where the employer pays the fee.
- Retained/executive search firms, where the company pays a retainer for the firm to work on the assignment and picks up search expenses.
- Contingency search firms, where the company pays the fee if and when a suitable candidate is hired (although expenses are occasionally charged).

The vast majority of successful placements are made under an arrangement whereby the company pays the fees. (Before you opt for anything else, ask yourself exactly what type of employees have to pay to find work.) Each of the major employer-paid categories performs a different service.

Employment agencies provide services similar to companies in the other two categories, but for the most part the employment agencies restrict their activities to the local job market. A traditional employment agency will not only actively recruit on your assignments, but will also do extensive advertising.

These firms are market-oriented, and will present the same candidate to you that they present to other interested parties. To avoid a bidding war for the best talent, move fast, refuse to get involved in salary-escalating games, and develop a good relationship with key players at the agencies of your choice. You may eventually win a measure of exclusivity when it comes to the best candidates.

The retained/executive search firm charges a retainer based on the first-year remuneration package, typically one-third on signing, one-third on presentation of the short list, and one-third on completion. Expenses are often pro-rated; there is no refund if the search is unsuccessful. Only you can say when this is, however: the search firm can be counted on to continue the assignment for a considerable period of time. Firms in this category will only present candidates to fill a specific assignment and opening; you won't hear about someone who may be right for you somewhere down the line.

These firms are most effective for those positions that pay over $100,000 yearly. A number of the better ones are members of the National Association of Corporate Professional Recruiters. (Note: many of the principals of companies in this area are surprisingly ignorant of some of the most basic employment laws. Do not assume you are hooking up with a competent expert in the field simply because you are paying a hefty retainer; shop around.)

The contingency search firm provides essentially the same services as the retained variety, but a fee is only paid by the employer upon successful completion of a search, and there is only occasionally an attempt to charge expenses. Clients frequently use more than one such firm at a time. Many of the companies in this category will present you with the opportunity to see candidates outside of the specific area you've requested for whom they feel you might have an interest. Contingency search firms are most effective with positions that range from $25,000 to $150,000.

This category makes up the single largest sector of the employment services community. With over 21,000 companies out there, the quality, as you might imagine, can vary dramatically from firm to firm.

So what type of employment services company is best for you? The one that will get you the right employees in the most professional and hassle-free manner. Every company has different needs; it may take some experimenting before you identify the company that "clicks."

With that in mind, let's examine a few myths that surround the employment industry. First of all, a retained executive search firm is not necessarily any better or more professional than any other employment firm. Each category has its exemplary practitioners and its charlatans. Your goal should be to establish good relations with a handful of firms within each of these categories. (You should also avoid antagonizing employment services people; you don't want your staff raided!)

Ask plenty of questions in your efforts to separate the employment services wheat from the chaff. How long has the firm been in business? What are the professional qualifications of both principal and individual consultants?

A company's involvement in professional associations is always a good sign. It demonstrates commitment and, since these associations usually offer extensive professional training programs, can indicate a greater degree of competence than you will find in other companies.

In the employment services industry, the National Association of Personnel Consultants is the premier professional organization, with state associations in all fifty states. Reputable retained and contingency firms and employment agencies are represented in the membership of this organization, which provides extensive training programs and maintains a strict code of ethics.

You should also ask if your contact has CPC designation, which stands for Certified Personnel Consultant. The international equivalent is the Certified International Personnel Consultant, or CIPC. CPC and CIPC designations, which represent the only professional accreditations in the field, are recognized as standards of excellence and commitment, and are only achieved after rigorous training and study. Even the newest holders of CPC designations will have approximately five years of experience, with the average running between seven and ten for all holders. (Note: It is to your advantage to find a CPC with experience in the particular field you are hoping to hire in. Not only will the communication be easier than with someone outside your field, but the contacts at your disposal will be better.)

Qualified CPCs can be relied upon to have superior knowledge of the legalities and ethics of the recruitment and hiring process, as well as the expertise that only comes from years of hands-on experience. Needless to say, these are advantages that you will want to have on your side during a search.

A listing of all current CPC designates who are also members of the National Association of Personnel Consultants is available in the *National Directory of Personnel Consultants by Specialization*, available for $19.95 plus $1.50 shipping and handling from:

National Association of Personnel Consultants
1432 Duke Street
Alexandria, Virginia 22314

Four: The Cracks in the Resume

The most important thing you should know about resumes is that they are like mirrors in a funhouse: They offer a distorted image of reality whose main function is to deceive the eye. Resumes have long been regarded as worth little more than the paper they are written on, but by learning how to decipher them, their value returns.

If you don't want to get fooled, your first job is to find the cracks the different resume types are designed to hide. As the accepted objective of a resume is to generate enough interest to get an interview, you would be prudent to assume that the writer will put anything down that will help get a foot in the door.

It is not accidental that resumes follow different formats. Depending on the person in question, one style will show work history and track record in a far better light than another. There are four styles of resume in common use, and each has different capabilities to highlight certain strengths and leave the skeletons well hidden in the closet. Let's open the door and have a look.

The Functional Resume & Broadcast Letter:

The functional resume is perhaps the most confusing to decipher. It focuses attention on major skills and specific accomplishments in certain areas. It provides no chronological record of employment and no detail of the type of jobs where this experience was gained.

The broadcast letter is similar to the functional resume, only less enlightening. It is comprised of four or five achievement-packed sentences, and is designed to knock you off your feet. It always finishes with a comment that you will receive a call in the next few days to set up a meeting.

Perfectly capable people with gaps in their employment history will use functional or broadcast techniques, as will contenders for the national job-hopping record. Of course, you should not eliminate these people from contention on that score alone, at least not until you know why they left each job and why there are gaps. If responsibilities with various employers grew each time, it may just signify a person of high competency and low boredom threshhold. All you may need to do is to keep this type of individual challenged.

High-powered, heavily experienced, and mature workers also are traditionally encouraged to use the functional or broadcast format. The common feeling among resume advisors is that the age, depth of experience, and concommitant cost of these people will deter many would-be employers. But that shouldn't be the main issue for you. We live in a youth culture where the cream of our workforce—pros in their 40's, 50's, and 60's—are being chucked onto the slag heap. Remember, they are the ones who have seen the problems before, who have extensive frames of reference for projection and anticipation, and who are more likely to have developed the habit of doing things right the first time rather than doing them over again. These people can be eminently desirable. By the same token, however, you will want to take their manageability carefully into account at the interview.

Folks with military, government, and educational backgrounds will often use these two styles of resume as well. Although they may have nothing to hide, there are big differences between the relatively protected lives they have led and the world of commercial business. Each one of these types, though, can be of real benefit to a company. I have noticed that ex-military officers, once they have adjusted to civvy street, can be a boon to the small, growing, or entrepreneurial company. They bring a great sense of order and method to a situation where it is often sorely needed. Just be sure you get one with the ability to treat subordinates with the courtesy and dignity necessary in civilian life. People from government and academia are used to working in political environments, where many opinions exist at once; their diplomacy can be helpful in a highly structured yet dynamic company.

Career-changers and those with diverse employment backgrounds are also fond of the functional and broadcast formats, to avoid tying their background to irrelevant jobs. With these styles, they can concentrate on general functional skills and achievements without being too specific. The achievements, not their employment history, will indicate a person of high drive and intelligence, to compensate for lack of relevant industry experience.

The Chronological Resume:

Chronological resumes are probably the most common and need the least explanation. Their set-up is exactly what it sounds, a chronological record of employment history. They are used by people who have no gaps in their history or who feel such gaps can be hidden by sleight-of-hand. This type of resume will often demonstrate successively responsible positions.

The Combination Resume:

The combination resume is from a mixture of both the functional and chronological styles. It is the most comprehensive, because it reveals both employment history and highlights specific skills and accomplishments. For my money, it is the most useful to you.

No matter which resume style is used, all job-hunters are told to list their achievements and to demonstrate how they helped previous employers. Very often, these claims are exaggerations of a modest truth. They come in three appealing categories, and look like this:

> *Money Earned for the Company:* This junior salesman not only sold more peanut butter than anyone else, but he also got the entire population of Maine to stand on their heads and gargle it. He would like to do the same for your company.
> *Money Saved for the Company:* This accountant saved her company from certain ruin by inventing the modern computer and reducing staffing needs in her department by 98%.
> *Time Saved:* This computer programmer designed a new program that reduced processing time by half, and that time saving is valued at $1.5 million so far this year.

The root of such claims is generally known as the Apollo Syndrome, after a low-level functionary at Cape Kennedy who claimed the success of the first Apollo mission as result of serving the coffee to the scientists, who otherwise would not have stayed awake long enough to get the ship launched successfully. He "provided key support to top scientists," etc. Although it is possible that we would all be twenty years behind if Einstein didn't get his coffee and had been unable to stay awake, do be especially aware of such phrases.

Sometimes the achievements claimed in resumes are 100% true, but at all times they are worthy of closer examination. The misrepresentation of job responsibilities has become perhaps the most substantial form of resume embellishment. Much of it is done with the use of dramatic action verbs: achieved, streamlined, managed, implemented, etc. Just because such words are in front of you on 22-pound rag paper does not make them true.

It is not so much that the writer is lying to you, but that many of the common action verbs have been so abused in their usage that they've become cliches. Still, it is easy for you, the manager, to misinterpret them. Take "reorganized" and "implemented" for example: "Implemented office reorganization" could be a rather grand way of saying, "I helped shift some desks around one slow Thursday afternoon." When you come across those action verbs, flag them for further examination. Taking the word "managed" as an example, whenever you see it in a resume, immediately highlight it and start asking yourself questions: How would this person define the difference between management and supervision? how long has he or she been in management, at what level, and how many people where managed? was management on a project basis or otherwise? did this person hire, fire, and perform salary and performance reviews? The questions that don't answer themselves in further examination of the resume, are the ones for which you will frame questions at the interview, to ensure that neither of you unwittingly deludes the other.

Keep a keen eye on all educational claims. Ph.Ds from impressive-sounding but obscure emporiums of higher education—such as the Pangalactic School of Business Management, Berne, Switzerland—should be red flags. Mail-order universities have even been known to be run from the corner table in Millie's Bar & Grill; in which case the Ph.D would stand for Pickled, high, and Drowsy. (Watch for my next book—I intend to byline myself as Dr. Yate.) Also, too much detail about the degree can mean that space is being filled up for lack of anything better to say.

Do not confuse credentials with accomplishments: You may have seen this confusion in others when they have elevated ineffective, degreed baboons to positions of authority, possibly in your own company. More valuable to you than a ten-year-old degree is evidence of additional courses or seminars attended that tell you prior employers felt it worthwhile to invest time and money in the individual—time and money, by the way, that won't have to come out of your pocket.

The Personalized Matching Sheet

Now while applicants have the right to show themselves in their best light, you still have to decide which ones you might want to see, which to disregard, and which to save for another occasion. It can be easier than you think if you create a personalized matching sheet:

- Take a sheet of paper and draw a line down the center.
- Consider the most important facets of the job and list them one beneath the other, down the lefthand side.
- Make a number of photocopies.

To use the matching sheet, just read through any of the resumes on your desk and jot down the person's relevant experience in the righthand column opposite the appropriate line. Because this technique makes the matches so obvious, it saves considerable time, frustration, and indecision.

Analyzing the Basics

Armed with the viable candidates from your matching sheets, you need to return to the resume and establish employment history and experience continuity. With each of the different resume styles, watch out for employment gaps. *Last-Chance Electronics 1980-1984*, then *Fly-By-Night Software 1984-Present* seems like a fair progression at first glance. But what if the candidate had left one company in January of 1984 and not joined the next one until December? You could have an employment gap of up to a year. And that means three things: Deception is being employed; there is one year less experience than at first assumed; and a similar amount of time has been spent professionally rusting rather than growing.

Unless you are wary about employment dates in the very beginning, your tendency will be to accept them on second reading as almost gospel. This results in the typical interviewer asking questions merely to confirm resume content, rather than examine and question it. This awareness will have you flagging annual employment dates with a marker to remind yourself to find out both the starting day, if possible, and month. Likewise you will be interested in learning the termination date and month for all jobs. Asking yourself these questions now will help you catch concealed employment gaps at the interview, and the revelation of such undesirable symptoms could be just what you need to lead you toward the right hiring decision.

Along with start and termination dates for successive jobs, you will want to learn about starting and leaving salaries. Often on a resume you will find no specific comments about salary, and at best, you are only likely to come across current earnings or desired earnings for the upcoming job. Nevertheless, learning about the candidate's salary progression can reflect his general industriousness, ability, and willingness to contribute.

With each identifiable job on the resume, you should be looking for answers to a set sequence of questions: On what date did this person start this job, and how much did he or she accept to start? on what date did he or she leave and how much was the salary at that point in time?

As questions about the past are less threatening and therefore more likely to get you truthful answers, get in the habit of asking yourself these questions with earlier jobs. The habit you form now will become second nature during their interview, and the result will be a candidate less likely to jump those 5% salary increases to 20%. Even if it does happen, you will be justified in questioning the sudden escalation in salary progression. Past habits predict future behaivor, and this habit of salary progression analysis will help you accurately predict the level of dollar offer the candidate will accept. This can save you the pain of losing a good employee through inadequate incentive or, alternatively, of showering the person with an unexpected embarrassment of riches.

As you ask yourself this question sequence about each job, it is only logical that questions about why the person left each job will spring to mind. This becomes especially interesting when there seems little upward mobility in the succession of jobs.

Reading resumes is no one's idea of a good time. After half a dozen, even the strongest wills among us begin to approach a state of catatonia. So do it in batch, reading a few at a time. Use this task as a break from your major duties; and thank your lucky stars that your resume isn't being subjected to worse treatment. If you've assigned others to do the screening of the resultant avalanche of paperwork, trot over once in a while and examine the ones that have been rejected. Doing this has a couple of benefits. One, it keeps you and your screeners on red alert. Two, every now and then you will find some interesting fish that were about to be thrown back into the swim. If you leave all the screening in other's hands, you have no one but yourself to blame when you are still looking come next budget allocation, or have settled on a less than perfect hire. The role of your internal screening agents is to provide you with a wide array of suitable choices, so make sure that you give them every assistance to do just that.

Fortunately, perhaps, there is no necessary connection between a resume's quality and that of the candidate. It is merely an advertisement of something that might be for sale with the right encouragement, and being a prudent consumer you will taste and try before you buy. But remember not to gorge yourself on resumes, or that razor-sharp mind will turn dull quickly. Look for the cracks, and remember that what is not said can be as revealing as what is.

Once you decide that a particular candidate is worth seeing, read through the resume again and jot down questions for any areas that you feel need clarification or probing. Do it now, when you are still objective and unaffected by personality impact. You'll be able to use these first impressions to formulate knock-out questions to be asked during the screening interview.

☙ *Five:* From Phoner to Short List

A while back, a corporate headhunter was discussing a potential V.P. of engineering with a Silicon Valley client. Among the many problems the headhunter was facing was one that simply couldn't be overcome: The client disagreed vehemently with the way the candidate's current employer had handled some business, and he was afraid the potential V.P. might bring some bad habits to the company. The headhunter felt certain that the candidate was perfect for the job—she'd been working on the assignment for seven months. So she told a lie. "Jack," she said to the company's C.E.O., "I am afraid I've made a mistake, and I hope you're going to feel able to get me off the hook." She explained that she had been so certain of the match that she had jumped the gun and already scheduled the candidate to call in about twenty minutes for a telephone interview—a "phoner." Would Jack do a favor by spending a few minutes on the phone with him, for appearance's sake? Jack obliged. The outcome? Jack and the candidate spent all the next day at a face-to-face meeting, and by 4 p.m., the candidate had been offered and had accepted the job. One thing I forgot to mention. The headhunter *hadn't* actually set up the phoner, but right after Jack had agreed to get her off the hook, she had called the recruit and said the C.E.O. was so excited that he wanted to speak to him immediately. Sometimes the end justifies the means.

The moral to the story is: A telephone call is worth a hundred objections, and if you aren't sure about an applicant's suitability, *get him or her on the phone.* With the techniques and questions from this chapter, you will be able to make a prudent decision quickly about a face-to-face meeting. The reason for this preliminary conversation is to gather and evaluate information that will help you in the winnowing process by quickly screening out the mismatches. Your only goal during a telephone interview should be to determine the essentials, so that you meet only the probable candidates. You shouldn't try to probe all the niceties of judgment, willingness, manageability, or the intangibles of personal chemistry over the telephone, for the simple fact that it's nearly impossible to do.

Using the telephone as the front-line of your screening process is helpful in other ways, too: For instance, when interviewing applicants from out of town, the cost of flying in any but the strongest candidates is prohibitive—and it is simply not fair to weaker candidates if, as is often the case at lower levels, they are footing the bill.

The telephone interview also solves the problem of having an enormous number of applicants to choose from. You can even use the process as a management tool. It's simple: Because the phoner is used mainly for fact-finding, you can assign the task to a competent individual on your staff, provide some initial interview training, and with clear instructions have that person verify all the flagged areas from the resume, paying special attention to employment dates, salary progressions, and reasons for leaving different employers. This way, you provide career development for a key employee while managing your precious time effectively. You can then use this verification of key areas as your stepping-stone to more pertinent areas of discussion, either in your half of the phoner or in a subsequent one. However you arrange it, the telephone interview reduces a long list of applicants to a short list of viable candidates; from now on, meeting any but the short-listers face to face should become obsolete. And, of course, it is also far easier, quicker, and less embarrassing to dismiss an also-ran over the phone than it is in person.

A telephone interview should be arranged in a manner convenient to both parties. A phone call to an applicant during business hours might cause some embarrassment for him or her, especially if the call has come in during a meeting with a superior! So when you do schedule a telephone interview during working hours, give the candidate the courtesy of initiating the call. After all, who has the bigger confidentiality problem? You might call first and diplomatically arrange your phone interview in a few moments, bearing in mind that the candidate may be limited to yes or no responses. This way, your candidate can ensure there is privacy before calling you, and you in turn will have a more responsive interviewee. Similarly, you may wish to conduct some of your telephone interviewing after normal business hours.

Phoner Questions

As the interviewer, you must take the lead in this "ritualistic dance." If you say too much, the interviewee has the time and necessary information to tailor his or her answer, to tell you what you want to hear. By being reticent, you allow the interviewee to show truer colors, to be, perhaps unwittingly, more honest.

Use this section to help plan specific questions ahead of time. The conversation must necessarily start with a few introductory words, but avoid the tendency to explain what you are looking for. Restrict yourself to a brief overview of the job in non-specific terms.

Once you have asked the basic questions you've built from the resume probe, your major goal becomes the determination of the applicant's capability. Focus your questions around the special skills and knowledge required to perform each of the major functions of the job by determining relative levels of experience.

"What kind of experience do you have?"

This is good for starters. It seeks *depth* of experience, rather than *amount*. Such a probe is far more effective than the traditional, "How much experience do you have?" where you may bamboozle yourself with quantity rather than with quality of experience. More than one manager over the years has discovered, to his or her loss, that ten years of experience is not always ten *progressive* years, but perhaps just the first two years repeated five times. Asking "kind" rather than "how much" will give you a qualitative rather than a quantitative answer. You will also notice that the phrasing of the question requires a response that can tell you a great deal more than a statement such as, "I have six years' experience," which, when you think about it, tells you very little.

"What aspects of your work do you consider most crucial?"

The answer to this will show the interviewee's grasp of functional responsibilities and may highlight how he or she prefers to spend time at work. In the answer, you must be alert for a potential mismatch. The personal secretary who does not regard the smoothing of a boss' path a crucial function may not be the right personal secretary for you. The matching here should be a simple matter of equating the interviewee's answers with the functional job description that you developed earlier.

"Of all the work you have done, where have you been most successful?"

This question follows smoothly from the last. It will demonstrate your interviewee's ability to contribute in those most crucial areas or will display an imbalance of efforts in the less than important areas. Taking this latter tendency to its utmost extreme, you could end up with employees who invest their time and energies in projects of their liking rather than yours.

"How necessary is it for you to be creative on your job?"

The appropriate response naturally depends on the position you are filling. Where the job requires strict adherence to policies and procedures, high degrees of creativity are often not desirable: Creativity in copywriters is desirable; in typists, it is not.

Knock-Out Questions

We next come to four examples of what I call knock-out questions—if you can't answer them, you are knocked out of consideration. You will see that they quickly determine whether the interivewee has a firm grasp of what it takes to do the job. In practice, this sequence has revealed some apparently desirable candidates to be dead from the neck up.

"What would you say are the broad responsibilities of [e.g.] a computer programmer?"

This question is carefully geared to be non-specific. As the interview cycle progresses, the questions will become increasingly subject-specific, but at this point in the proceedings, you are simply trying to get a focus on the big picture. The answer you receive provides a clear indication of the interviewee's understanding of the general functions and responsibilities of someone in this position. Additionally, the interviewee will be telling to you what his or her perceived limits of responsibility are and also how he or she perceives the position's relationship and interaction with other positions and departments.

"What would you say are the major qualities this job demands?" or, *"What would you say are the traits a good [e.g.] computer programmer would possess?"*

These are both questions with the same intent but different wording. Behind them both is an awareness that every job has its good and bad points, and that every job demands certain qualities of its acolytes and excludes others. For instance, over-sensitive salespeople rarely make the grade—and we have yet (to our chagrin) to find an I.R.S. auditor heavy with the milk of human kindness. In developing the job description, you have already identified the specific traits necessary to be successful in this position, so an answer that is way off base should raise a red flag.

"Describe to me how your job relates to the overall goals of your department and company."

This one is really not so obscure as it might first appear. In this day and age, everyone should know that a company is in business to make a profit, and is not running a social club to keep the feeble-minded off the streets. Consequently, the interviewee who is alert to how his or her individual efforts fit into the big corporate picture is liable to be more interested, involved, and motivated in the work than one who hasn't a clue. And anyone who does not understand how his or her job contributes to the success of the company is going to be less concerned for its well-being.

Likes and Dislikes

Having started with a broad determination of functional capabilities, then moved to an evaluation of the interviewee's grasp of the big picture, we now bring the questioning into sharp focus on the interviewee's likes and dislikes. While these questions have been traditionally asked at the face-to-face interview, they are so effective in unmasking mismatches that they can be used during the telephone interview for their knock-out qualities.

The questions here (and, for that matter, throughout the chapter) gather valuable information without defining your needs or letting the interviewee tell you merely what you want to hear. These questions focus on an individual's broad ability to take the rough that goes with the smooth in every job: Carol and Sheldon might have great voices and good telephone personalities, but if they have short tempers or are easily ruffled, you would not want to hire them as a customer service managers dealing with inquiries and complaints.

"What would you change about your current job?" and, *"What aspects of it do you like least?"*

These questions should be asked in conjunction, for their answers can bring interesting data to light, and knock someone out if the "changes" and "least-likes" don't mesh with your most critical functions and "must-haves." And no matter how qualified, someone who has problems with one of your "must-haves" is obviously not suitable for your job and should be rejected now: Job distraction can lead only to fast turnover.

"What aspects of your job do you like best?"

This question connects the dots in the like/dislike area. It will also occasionally reveal that what a potential employee likes most is the "busy work" connected with the job. We have all seen those individuals, who seem to work like Trojans all the work-long day but never seem to get anything done; they are task-oriented rather than goal-completion-oriented. So, the question helps reveal good potential matches with your candidates when the most favored areas closely match your needs.

"What are the most repetitive tasks in your job?"

This is the first part of a two-part question. Learn again whether the work experience matches your requirements, and what areas the interviewee may find a little boring. The second part is, *"How do you handle them?"* Notice that you ask it in two parts to avoid giving the interviewee any guidance toward the type of response desired.

"What are you looking for in your next job?"

This one fits in comfortably here or might easily find its way into the conversation while you are verifying employment and salary history. In the interviewee's answer, you will be alert for a match between the candidate's needs for the future and what your opening can genuinely provide. A match will give the candidate job satisfaction and give you, therefore, a motivated and content employee. The further apart the interviewee's desires are from your ability to provide, the smaller your chances of maintaining a long-term working relationship together.

"What kind of things bother you most about your job?"

With the answer to this, you must remember to compare it honestly with the job's realities. Just imagine hiring a receptionist who hated being rushed or loathed the sound of ringing bells.

Money

Money makes for good specific questions. It is also a topic that should always be addressed first on the telephone, because it is foolhardy to waste time and money conducting a face-to-face meeting when there is a serious fiscal imbalance.

"How much money are you making?"

This is fine for starters, and better if you come back to it after having verified the rest of the salary history. You might expect a little fudging on earnings; everyone has done it at one time or another. If you do feel that the salary seems high, follow up with, *"What I am really looking for is your salary, not the value of your benefit package or other fringes."* This will often bring the individual back on track and also provide a graceful exit from a potentially awkward situation.

"How much money do you want?"

Although at this point this is somewhat of an unfair question, it might not be a bad idea to get the chance to test poise and quick thinking under pressure. Alternatively, you could hold the question (and phrase it differently) until all of your other questions have been answered. You should of course be prepared for the occasional response, "That depends on the job. How much are you paying?" Then you might wish to describe the overall (but not detailed) responsibilities of the job and follow them with the following question:

"In your professional opinion, how much do you think a job like this should pay?"

As the hiring manager, you are never under obligation to reveal your salary range, and such a response puts the ball neatly back in the interviewee's court.

"What else should I know about your qualifications for this job?" or, *"What else should I know about you?"* or, *"Is there anything else you want to tell me?"*

Such questions are clear signals to the interviewee that the conversation is drawing to a close, and that it is the last opportunity for the candidate to bring forth or emphasize any strengths or relevant experience. You may even discover hidden talents that the course of the interview has not revealed. At least, you will reassure yourself that nothing valuable has been missed.

The Verdict

By the end of the interview you will have reached one of these conclusions:

The applicant is not able to do the job. If this is the case, you will let the applicant down gently. It is common courtesy, and though he or she is inappropriate today, this same person could be right for tomorrow's opening. You can say, "Competition is fierce. I have others to talk to, and I feel that you may not make the short list for this particular position. However, you have some unique skills, and I would like to keep you in mind for the future."

You are still not sure. Tell the person how you feel (we can all handle the truth) and suggest that while you are considering the matter, the applicant may want to write you a letter emphasizing his or her relevant strengths. You might say, "Competition is keen, and I have others to talk to. I'm not sure at this point whether you will make the short list, but I have to give it further consideration. Would you be willing to write me a letter detailing your strengths? It could help." This additional test will also define determination, interest, and written communication skills.

The applicant is able and possibly willing. Therefore, the applicant is someone you will want to talk to. Now it is time to schedule a face-to-face meeting and plan your approach (using the rest of *Hiring the Best*) so that you will be able to evaluate not only ability and willingness to do the job, but also manageability, judgment, and those intangibles of personal chemistry necessary to fit into the team. Set the ground rules:

- You expect all appointments to be kept punctually
- You expect to be informed if for any reason a candidate cannot make a meeting
- You will treat any and all information shared with you as confidential

- You expect application forms to be filled out accurately and completely.
- You intend to check references

People always respect what you inspect. These statements (especially the one about checking references) will encourage honesty from the beginning of the face-to-face interview.

As much as the pressures of real world allow, bunch all your telephone interviews together over a day or two, so that you are able to compare candidates objectively with one another. Once that short list of the most viable has been made, you will want to prepare for each meeting and each conversation. Chapter Six, "The Art and Science of Interviewing," will help you do just that.

☙ *Six:* The Art and Science of Interviewing

Those relaxed and casual conversations you see on the television talk shows are deceptive in their appearance; hours of careful preparation are involved, as are years of practice and technique development. The same effort must apply to developing your own interviewing style. The competent interviewer is far more than someone who has a long string of questions to ask each candidate; the competent interviewer is someone who understands the art and science of interviewing.

F. Lee Bailey, arguably the greatest courtroom performer of our day, talks of going into court with 50 rabbits in his hat, and not knowing which he will need. This charismatic performer is ready with them all. He's ready with multiple approaches and questioning techniques; he is attentive to detail. F. Lee Bailey usually wins.

You have your day in court whenever you interview a potential new employee; you are defending your livelihood and your standing as a competent manager. Here are all the rabbits you will need to be ready for every interviewing situation.

The Art of the Question

Gathering information is the key to competent interviewing, and nothing is more important than an ability to be flexible in your questioning techniques; you must do it so smoothly that no one realizes it but you. A questioning style that is appropriate in one instance may give you false, misleading, or—worse still—no information at all in another instance. The following twelve techniques will help you ring the changes as the situation demands and ensure that you strike the right note every time.

Closed-Ended Questions:

These are the most commonly asked questions in interviewing, and also the most commonly abused. How often have you heard of interviewers asking a closed-ended question such as, "Can you work under pressure?" Only yes and no are the possible answers (and who answers no?). The interviewer has no information, no way of evaluating any one candidate against another. But while a closed-ended question is inappropriate in its most common usage, it is useful as a questioning technique when you are looking for commitment ("Can you start on Monday?") or when you are refreshing your memory or verifying information from earlier in the interviewing sequence ("You were with Xerox for ten years?"). You can also use it to get the ball rolling when you have a series of questions on the same subject.

Open-Ended Questions:

These questions are logically the opposite of the first questioning technique. With an open-ended question, the interviewee cannot get by with a monosyllablic answer; instead the question demands an explanation in response. For example, "How do you succeed in working under pressure?" is an open-ended question that asks the interviewee to answer in detail. As a rule of thumb, this style of question is preferable to closed-ended questions, and is guaranteed to keep the candidate talking and you listening.

These questions often start with, "I'm interested in hearing about ... " "I'm curious to learn ... " "Would you share with me ..."

Past-Performance Questions:

This technique has been developed into a whole style of interviewing (discussed later). Past-performance, or behavioral, questions are based on the premise that past actions can predict future behavior, that any given individual can be expected to do as least as well or as badly on the new job as he or she did on the last. They are open-ended by nature, yet focus on requesting specific examples of past behavior. They are usually prefaced with, "Tell me about a time when . . . " "Share with me an experience when . . . " "Give me an example of . . . " Ask past-performance questions early in the interview, so that an interviewee will realize early on that he or she is expected to give detailed examples about the past and will be less tempted to try pulling the wool over your eyes as the interview progresses.

Negative-Balance Questions:

When interviewing, you can be tempted all too often to believe that a candidate strong in one area is equally impressive in all areas. This is not always the case. When an eerie light appears around the applicant's head, and hymns from a choir of heavenly angels replace the background noise of your office's typewriters, it is time to get a grip on yourself and look for the applicant's feet of clay. Whenever you find yourself becoming unduly impressed, try, "That's very impressive. Was there ever an occasion when things didn't work out quite so well?" or the simple, "Now give me an example of something in this area you are not so proud of?"

Negative Confirmation:

When you have sought and found negative balance, you may feel content that you are maintaining your objectivity and move on, or that the answer you receive may be disturbing enough to warrant negative confirmation. Let's say the interviewee told you about a time she found it necessary to go around or behind her supervisor to achieve a goal. As a manager, you will be given considerable pause: If such behavior is common with this individual, you would be unwise to invite her onto your team. Consequently, you will seek negative confirmation with, "You know that's very interesting. Let's talk about another time when you had to . . . " Successive examples will help you confirm negative traits and perhaps save you from a poor hire. On the other hand, you might find that particular negative situation to be an aberration, a one-time thing, and nothing to worry about.

Reflexive Questions:

Reflexive questions are great topic-closers and conversation-forwarders. They help you calmly maintain control of the conversation no matter how loquacious the interviewee. If, for instance, an applicant starts to ramble about various experiences, it is easy to interrupt with a reflexive question that will allow you to proceed with other topics. This is done by adding don't you? couldn't you? wouldn't you? didn't you? can't you? aren't you? to the end of a statement. For example: "With time so short, I think it would be valuable to move onto another area, don't you?" The candidate's reflex is to agree, and the conversation moves on.

Mirror Statements:

This is a subtle form of probing used in conjunction with that most effective tool, silence. The technique is to mirror or paraphrase a key statement and follow it by closing your mouth, nodding, and looking interestedly at the interviewee.

Use mirror statements to capture the essence of a candidate's answer and to get more detail. Repeat the substance of key comments ("So, whenever you are two hours late for work, you take off two hours early to make up for it"), then sit and wait for the interviewee to expand on the mirror statement.

Loaded Questions:

Loaded questions are much abused because they can allow the interviewer to play power games. The question style requires the interviewee to decide between tough options. For instance: "Which do you think is the lesser evil, embezzlement or forgery?" There is, however, a very fine line between absurd loaded questions and carefully balanced judgment-call questions. For most interviewers, the technique is useful to probe the interviewee's decision-making approaches. The easiest and most effective way to employ it is to recall a real-life situation where two divergent approaches were both carefully considered; then frame the situation as a question, starting with, "I'm curious to know what you would do if . . . " or, "What would be your approach to a situation where . . . "

Half-Right Reflexive:

This question style is used to smoke out yes-men, the incurably incompetent, the oddballs who have a total resistance to giving information, and the competent but incurably tongue-tied. The technique is to make a statement that is only partially correct and ask the interviewee to agree. It is astounding what enlightening insights this technique can create. For instance: "I've always felt that customer service should start only after the bill has been paid, haven't you?" This example of the half-right reflexive always generates fascinating responses.

Leading Questions:

Here, you lead the listener toward a specific type of answer. These questions often arise accidentally as a result of the interviewer explaining what type of company the interviewee will be joining. The interviewer might proudly explain, "We're a fast-growing outfit here, and there is constant pressure to meet deadlines and satisfy your ever-increasing list of customers," then ask, "How do you handle stress?" The interviewee knows that to retain any chance of landing an offer he or she must answer a certain way and consequently does so. This is not to say that leading questions are inadvisable, but like closed-ended questions, they must be used appropriately. Their best use is as information verifiers, to get the candidate to expand on a particular topic. For example: "We are a company that believes the customer is always right. How do you feel about that?" But you should use the technique only once the candidate's belief or performance in a particular area has been established. In either case, leading questions should not be used early in the interview or confused with the somewhat sophisticated half-right reflexive.

Question Layering:

A good question poorly phrased will loose its bite and give you incomplete or misleading information, but question layering can probe an answer thoroughly and on many levels. Let's start with the earlier example of wanting to know whether a potential employee can work under pressure. Many interviewers would simply ask, "Can you work under pressure?" and while the intent is good, the question style is wrong for several reasons (as mentioned before): The question requires only a yes or no answer, which tells you nothing; and it leads the interviewee toward the type of answer he or she knows you want to hear.

Instead, you should take a leaf out of a good reporter's notebook. The reporter uses all the styles we have discussed, but in a way that peels back different layers of truth until a topic has been examined from every angle: The reporter asks who, what, why, when, where, and how. In this instance, you do the same thing by joining the closed-ended question with some of the other questioning. See how much more relevant information you can glean:

"Can you work under pressure?" (Closed-Ended)
"Tell me about a time when you had to work under pressure."(Open-Ended)
"So, it was tough to meet the deadline?" (Mirror Statement)
"How did this pressure situation arise?"
"Who was responsible?"
"What did you do?"
"Why was this allowed to occur?"
"Where did the problem originate?"

Now you have eight different angles to the same question, each revealing a different aspect of the personality, performance, and behavior of your candidate. Nearly every question in this book can be given the layering treatment. In fact, this technique makes the possibilities for questions theoretically endless; it just depends on how thorough you want to be.

Remember: You should not accept a candidate's first answer to any of your questions. You have a right to look closer and check for cracks. If you feel something is lacking in an answer, pursue it by layering your questions. You'll never know unless you ask.

Hamburger-Helper Questions:

Just as people will sometimes use a little hamburger helper to make the ground beef go a little further, so you can use these three techniques to stretch a question.

1) If you are either dissatisfied with the first answer and want more data, or are so fascinated with the answer that you want to hear more, say, "Give me some more detail on that. It's very interesting," or, "Can you give me another example?"

2) You may hear an answer and add after it, "What did you learn from that experience?" This is an excellent layering technique that can give you a handle on judgment and emotional maturity, as well as give you more thinking and planning time.

3) Perhaps the best technique for gathering more information is simply to sit quietly, looking at the interviewee and saying nothing. All mankind is embarrassed by a conversational lull. Remember the last cocktail party you attended, when the silence lasted just a couple of seconds and was terminated by two or three people talking at once? This human frailty can be used to your advantage during the interview: The interviewee thinks, "Well, he's not saying anything, so he must be expecting me to say something else. I must not have finished my answer to his satisfaction." Even as the interviewer, you will find a little silence in the interview difficult to manage at first, but it can pay substantial dividends in the long run.

The Art of the Conversation

A wise person once said that people never really listen, but merely wait for their turn to speak. This universal truth can be used to your advantage during the interview. Once you learn the handful of techniques that keep the interviewee talking and you evaluating, your interviewing style will take on more of the feel of a conversation.

Living by the 80/20 Rule:

During the interview, ask questions 20% of the time and you will be able to listen 80% of the time. Each moment you are talking, valuable evaluation time is lost, and the subsequent lack of data on which to base your decision is the predictable outcome of the incompetent interviewer who fails to plan his or her questions. Know in advance what you are going to say and ask, and you will be able to dedicate the greater part of your time to listening.

Asking a person to justify or to expand on an answer is a useful tool that gives you evaluation time, especially so if you have become momentarily tongue-tied or are trying to analyze a prior response. "Why" or "Tell me more about that" help you live by the 80/20 rule and gather information while the interviewee talks.

Most managers break this rule by commenting on a candidate's answers. Not only does your editorializing take up time, it can also show the candidate where your priorities lie and encourage answers that reflect *your* values, not the candidate's. Don't show signs of agreement or disagreement; don't comment at all, unless it specifically serves your purpose. Just plug along pleasantly.

Framing Questions:

The candidate needs to concentrate on answering your questions, not deciphering them, so use easily understood words and keep the questions simply framed. Don't string too many questions or themes together in one breath. Unframed questions sound something like this: "Tell me about what kind of people you like to work with, what kind of people you don't like to work with, and how you get along with them." On the one hand, this type of questioning can be confusing to some candidates and agitate an otherwise smooth conversation; on the other, it will lead some candidates toward a "desirable" answer.

Sequencing Themes:

Ask your questions in themes and tie the changing themes smoothly together to provide continuity. For example: "Good, now that we have established you are a graduate of the Genghis Khan School of Business Management, let's talk about employee turnover."

Keeping the Interviewee on Track:

Remember that the person asking the questions in any conversation controls and directs its flow. As the interviewer and the applicant's possible future manager, you should establish that control now. Otherwise, the candidate may find ways to hide vital information you need or to direct the conversation away from your aims. If you ask a chemical engineer what personal qualities he or she thinks are necessary for success in the field, and get an answer like, "Well, you need at least three years' experience and an up-to-date knowledge of recent chemical patents," then you've received an answer to the wrong question. Put the interviewee back on track by being gently persistent: "I'm sorry, I meant what *personal* qualities, not what kind of experience."

Handling the Flustered Candidate:

Often during the interview, a candidate will be stumped on a question, and then the interviewer, from a mixture of embarrassment, awkwardness, and common fellow feeling, will let the candidate off the hook with, "That's all right, let's move on." This is the wrong way to go about it. Never let a candidate off the hook if he or she is experiencing difficulty in answering your question. It sets a bad precedent for the interview and for your future management of this person. Whenever this difficulty arises, look the candidate in the eye and say, "That's all right. Take your time to answer. I'm sure something will come." And sure enough, it will. Just sitting quietly and looking at the candidate will encourage more talking.

Don't be a blank wall, though; use silence judiciously. And be careful not to nail a candidate early on with this technique. He or she may become too nervous to proceed. If the candidate is severely stumped for an answer, back off before the trauma gets intense and the interview becomes an exercise in futility. It is okay to do this to maintain the flow of conversation, as long as you make a mental note to come back to the topic later when the candidate is more settled.

Handling the Talkative Candidate:

When the interviewee insists on chattering away to no real end, your challenge is not so much keeping the conversation going as stemming its flow once in a while and then redirecting it. Difficult as this problem has seemed to many people over the years, it really can be handled very easily and pleasantly. There are two ways of handling the overtalkative candidate:

1) Jump into the conversation with, "You know, that's very interesting. It makes me want to ask you about . . . " and then move on to the topic of your choice. 2) Start talking along with the candidate and redirect the conversation to a new area. Keep talking until the candidate shuts up, which will be in the first few seconds.

Do bear in mind, however, that if you consider hiring this candidate, you might have problems over the coming years getting a word in edgeways in your own department.

Master these conversational gambits, and the conversational flow of your interviews will always go the way you want and divulge the information you need.

The Science of Interviewing Styles

Today there are four fashionable interview styles: Situational, Personality Profile, Stress, and Behavioral. Each style has its adherents and its strengths. Yet, despite claims to the contrary, none can stand alone as the one and only way to interview.

Situational:

Situational interviewing is based on the theory that the closer you can get to a real work situation, the better your evaluation will be. You take candidates on a tour of the workplace as an integral part of the proceedings, but not just to fill in time. You will also get them actually to perform some aspect of the job. You stand by the machinery with the engineer and discuss it; you have the typist type a letter; you ask the accountant to analyze a balance sheet with some obvious mistakes built in; you put the telemarketer on the phone with you and role-play a difficult call.

A magazine publisher I know sets great store by this method. He uses a telemarketing department to sell his advertising space and always takes potential salespeople to the work area and discusses their job there. His payoff comes on the return to the quiet of his private office when he asks, "Well whadya think?" and gets such revealing answers as "Wow, I had no idea they made so many phone calls. Are they always on the phone like that?" He claims that no amount of questioning can get you such unconsidered gut reactions from job candidates.

As a corporate management trainer by trade, I was once surprised by being submitted to situational interviewing techniques myself. At an interview for a management training job, I was shown around the corporate training center, and the tour finished with the my interviewer and me standing by the flip charts and overhead projector. "How do you think you'd like training here?" asked the interviewer innocently. "Fine," I said, unaware of what was to follow. "Great. Then to get a feel of what it will be like, why don't you teach me something? I'll take a seat over here. Take five minutes and teach me anything you want." Afterward, I reviewed what had happened. There I was, a top trainer being put through my paces. No amount of probing and reference-checking could give the interviewer quite the same taste for my platform skills as seeing those skills in action; plus it allowed the interviewer to see whether I had a style compatible with the fabric of the corporation. As an interviewer, situational ploys can get you closer to the real job than almost any other technique. A good method but not perfect on its own.

Personality Profile:

This style of interviewing helps you find key personality traits—the traits so important to the success of each individual job. You will find out whether that salesperson talks a good game but in reality is too thin-skinned to be selling encyclopedias door-to-door. Many personality profile questions probe judgment and emotional maturity; others check the interviewee's general awareness of your corporate value systems versus the instant gratification of their own needs. This approach is effective but has defects if used alone.

Stress:

The constant barrage of tough, trick, and negatively phrased questions that constitute stress interviewing is designed to keep the candidate off balance, while the interviewer evaluates poise and quick thinking under pressure. Depending on the type of job, this can be a penetrating style. For example, if you are filling P.R. positions for the nuclear or chemical industries, stress questioning is probably useful and even necessary. In speaking with the manager of a Washington, DC television talk show, I heard a revealing story about such questions. A T.V. anchor position is a very stressful job: A million things can go wrong and often do. It is the anchor's task to remain calm and collected under fire, to be the epitome of that old adage, "the show must go on." One interviewer, who screened all staff for studio jobs, would end each interview with a promising candidate by saying, "We really are not sure you are suitable for the job." One young woman, who up to that point was a sure top contender, revealed her true colors by getting up and saying, "Well, I'm not sure I want to work here anyway." She showed herself to be someone who couldn't handle the pressure the job called for.

For general use, stress questioning can be effective but easily abused; it can also backfire on the interviewer. A candidate may come through with flying colors, be offered the job and flatly refuse it. A senior executive once said about a job offer from a dyed-in-the-wool stress interviewer, "I wouldn't work for that socially unacceptable S.O.B. on a bet." And remember that there is little point in using stress techniques if the employee will not be faced with undue stress on the job: Computer programmers and mailroom clerks are hardly in the same stress category as anchorpersons. Again, this technique can be effective when used appropriately, but it's not perfect.

Behavioral Interviewing:

This style of interviewing applies the leopard-never-changes-its-spots philosophy, bases all questions in the past, and requires the interviewee to give specific examples from work history. The belief that an individual will do at least as well on the new job as he or she has done in the past is often a reasonable assumption. Past behavior can predict future actions. A very effective style but, again, not perfect.

So which method do you use? Each method has something to offer, yet none is perfect. Additionally, interviewees rapidly become acclimatized to a particular approach: Throw nothing but negatively-phrased stress questions at a candidate, for example, and they soon lose their bite; consistently ask questions about a person's past performance, and the average interviewee quickly learns the rules of the game. The same applies to the situational and personality profile approaches. What is the sophisticated interviewer to do?

The sensible approach is to take the best aspects of each style and combine them to produce a comprehensive strategy, a sum greater than its parts. You will evaluate behavior, profile personality, weigh emotional maturity and judgment, and determine manageability. Your approach will allow time for the inclusion of situational techniques and the opportunity to test poise with some dastardly stress questions. This is the all-embracing approach set forth in *Hiring the Best* and the approach we will soon be examining.

Setting the Stage

Managers who build teams that can conquer any problem or bounce back from any setback are, first and foremost, competent interviewers. While the incompetents merely set out with the goal of determining whether a candidate can do the job, the good manager realizes that probing for ability is just *one* of the interview's multiple goals.

As a successful manager, you must take the extra steps that guarantee successful hires. Once you have determined the ability to do the job, you move on to evaluate willingness, because you understand the ocean of difference between able and willing, and don't wish to drown in it. You continue the process by analyzing the candidate's judgment, looking for emotional maturity, and probing the various aspects of his or her personality profile; in short, you decide whether the person could be manageable by you.

Meeting these multiple goals takes careful planning. No one discovers the solution to these complex considerations without having a plan of attack, a plan that will give you a systematic coverage of work history, job-related skills and ability to do the job. The plan that will allow you to gather all the facts about willingness, judgment, personality, and manageability. You will want to do this in a way that gives a uniformity and objectivity to evaluating all those who make it to your short list.

Building a plan of attack—giving structure to interview procedure—is the key to your success. And once you have planned your basic structure, you will furnish it with some of the carefully selected and sequenced questions from the following chapters. Fortunately, there is an easy way to create the basic structure to your interviews, without restricting your personal style or chosen techniques.

Setting the Tone

The employment interview is an unnatural, phony, and uncomfortable affair. Now, if it is all these things for you, what's it like for the poor devil sweating in the lobby, who is now recalling, remorsefully, that dinner last night was a little heavy on the garlic? Understanding the psychological state of the interviewee, and controling it for the ultimate benefit of both parties, are the keys to your success.

The substantial tension experienced by the candidate is created by the very nature of the decision about to be made. Every job candidate, at some level, feels that the acceptance/rejection decision soon to be handed down is based on his or her validity as a person.

The first meeting is a two-way street. Not only should you plan your evaluation campaign, you must also make the candidate want to turn that first meeting into a long-term relationship. The assumption that someone applying for a job is desperate to work for you and that you therefore have unilateral discretion is simply wrong. If the candidate is good, you can expect the same treatment you are giving; the individual, like you, is shopping around for the best deal. So while you are evaluating things from across the desk, the candidate does the same thing. You must have the ammunition ready to sell the job, the company's training, and the prospects for the future, when the need arises. It is helpful to remember that the things that first attracted *you* to the company could well appeal to someone else in your profession.

So, to know how to treat the job candidate, just turn the tables and think of yourself: What treatment would make *you* eager to join a company?

First and foremost, make the candidate comfortable and relaxed as early and as quickly as you can. It's not so much part of wooing as it is part of not getting fooled: It's more likely that a person treated in a warm and friendly manner from the start will respond to questioning in an open and honest manner than someone with the defenses up.

First impressions are indelible, and you can make a positive or negative impression before you ever meet your short-list of candidates. Does the front desk know that you are expecting someone? How are interviewees normally treated on arrival at your company? The tension a candidate feels at these times can be blown out of all proportion by a poor reception: "Oh yeah, another lamb to the slaughter, gas-chamber seats are over there." Creating the right impression in the lobby, however, will ensure that the candidate has already got a picture of your company as a good place to be. If the receptionist says, "Good morning Ms./Mr. Jones. We were expecting you. May I offer you some refreshment?" it will go a long way to creating a warm feeling. Every staff member who comes in contact with potential employees should be trained to treat them as welcome guests.

The same concept applies to you when greeting the candidate. It is conceivable that you could impress someone with your importance by sending a minion to lead the way to your castle, while you spend the time rearranging your desk to look busy. I've even observed senior executives (who should know better) hold important discussions with a dial tone in an effort to impress. But making the right impression takes no more effort and is no different than using the same good manners you exercise when welcoming a visitor to your home. Meet the candidate in the lobby yourself if you possibly can, and offer a sincere welcome.

Look the candidate in the eye. Give a firm handshake and say, "Hi, I'm pleased to meet you, Mr./Ms. Jones, and I'm looking forward to getting to know you better." If it hasn't been done yet, offer something to sip—coffee, tea, water. With interview nerves and dry mouths, such a gesture will be greatly appreciated.

The way you dress and the look of your office tell the candidate about your self-image and how seriously you are taking the interview. Neatness is the main thing. Much has been written about the interview environment, including tripe like, "Set a relaxed atmosphere. Don't interview across a desk. It sets a barrier. Instead, sit in easy chairs across a low coffee table." I'm not saying this isn't correct, really. But such advice *is* tripe for most of us because it is impractical: We mostly live in tiny cluttered cubicles full of file cabinets. So much for the dream of a paperless office that makes room for the easy chairs. We'll have a paperless bathroom first.

Anyway, if you can't snatch some more senior executive's plush office for your interview, just make sure that you have some privacy. It is unacceptable to either of you to be overheard during this meeting of minds.

Make sure you have all the relevant information about the job in one file: Job description, employment conditions, salary spreads, benefits, job prospects, questions. You will have to answer some questions yourself, and ignorance and unpreparedness do not build confidence in the potential employee. The interview should always begin with a little small talk to relax the candidate. Following close on the heels of this chit-chat, explain your goals but don't give the game away. Remain specifically vague. Emphasize that you will want get to know both the professional and the person and that you will also give the individual an opportunity to get his or her own questions answered.

Benefit Statement and Interview Outline

Proceed with a non-specific outline and benefit statement. "We are looking for a ________, and I want to learn about your experience and the strengths you can bring to our team. You can give me the best picture by being completely open and whenever possible give me specific examples from current or past jobs."

Tell the candidate that you are well prepared, that you have a lot of questions to ask. Explain that you will be taking notes to be sure this candidate's image stays fresh in your mind while you interview others and make your evaluation. (And having said so, do take notes!) Make clear that you intend to check references and salaries. Making the announcement helps to create an atmosphere of honesty; people respect what you inspect, not what you expect. And it makes perfect sense for you to double-check, to make sure that you understand as many dimensions of the candidate's history as you can.

Job History

This is the time when you concentrate on the can-do aspects of the job (see Chapter Seven). Use the resume or company application as the framework on which to base your questions, but do not regard the paperwork as the gospel truth; it is there merely as a basis for discussion. For the most part, these are the easy-to-ask, easy-to-answer questions that allow both of you to get used to talking with each other, and the candidate to get used to the idea that you are very thorough in your inspection of credentials.

☙ Performance Probing

This is the key part of the interview process where you probe the areas of willingness, emotional maturity, judgment, manageability, and personality (see Chapters Nine and Ten). Each dimension will be customized, of course, to the particular needs of your opening. If you are going to use some situational interviewing techniques or stress techniques, this is where you do it. With performance probing, you will have identified key areas to be examined before the interview and prepared specific question sequences from the following chapters designed to reveal the information you need.

There are two terrible places to be during an interview: Sitting in front of the desk, as the interviewee, wondering what is going to happen next; and sitting behind the desk, wondering the same damn thing. If you feel that way as an interviewer, don't panic: You are on the path to enlightenment. The path has four steps, the first being that of the unconscious incompetent: The interviewer who doesn't know that he or she doesn't know how to interview, and who looks at a face-to-face meeting as a chance "to get to know" the person. The second step is that of the conscious incompetent: The interviewer who knows that there is more to interviewing than he or she first realized, and who commits to increasing his or her knowledge. The third step toward satori is that of the conscious competent: The person who knows what he or she is doing every step of the way, who does not wear the mask of self-deception, and who plans each action in advance. The final state of bliss? That of the unconscious competent: When stage three has become second nature, and you no longer remember what it was like to stumble along wondering what question you should ask next and what you would do with the information if you got it anyway. You are on the path to satori.

Seven: Ability

The job description for the position you have open has various requirements, and you must judge whether the candidate can handle them—whether the candidate is able. Ability has one criterion: Does the candidate have a performance history that will let him or her function appropriately, even outstandingly, in the position? You will have to discover a few things: In his or her last jobs, what were the basic responsibilities? what sorts of achievements were made? what part did he or she play, and how well was it played, in the department and company? is his or her preparation sufficient for the job at hand?

The meat of an interview starts with getting this honest reading of employment history. What was the person's functional responsibility and ability in each of those positions? is the candidate therefore functionally suitable for the job you have in mind? You should start off with questions that are easy both to ask and to answer: It helps the interviewee to relax and you to hit your interviewing stride. Only when the interviewee is relaxed can you start throwing the curve-ball questions aimed at getting through to the hidden truth. If you start in with tough questions, your candidate's defenses will never come down.

The past is less threatening for the interviewee than the present, so begin with questions about earlier jobs. That way, you will be more likely to get truthful, straightforward answers. Then, as your questions gradually approach the present, the interviewee will have established a pattern of honesty, a habit that is hard for the interviewee to break, and easier for you to identify if it is broken.

Each manager's situation is unique, so there is no proper sequence to follow, no one revealing, streamlined set of questions to ask. You will naturally mix and match the questions in *Hiring the Best* to suit your particular needs; you will also have to put them into your own voice. The question sequences in this and following chapters have been organized to proceed logically, but are in no way intended as anything but broad guidelines for your benefit.

Basic Responsibilities

This first sequence of questions examines the key areas of a candidate's functional responsibilities. You will gain insight into skills, special knowledge, and relative strengths and weaknesses. This particular sequence can be repeated as required through every job the candidate has held. The cumulative result will be a clear picture of the candidate's essential capabilities. You may have asked some of these questions during the telephone interview, but it doesn't hurt to go over them again in greater detail, especially as they concern the candidate's current job. It can be used as a check-and-balance mechanism, and will also let you speed smoothly to your interview stride.

"What was the date you joined the company?"

This question will be followed by, *"What was your title when you joined the company?"* and, *"What was your starting salary?"* Together, these three questions help to set a tone for the meeting. They show that you are going to interview the candidate in detail and that you intend to get specific answers to specific questions. Immediately, the candidate will realize that you are someone who expects, and has the tools to get, the facts. Your most valuable data will come from the last seven years or three jobs, whichever comes first. Beyond these three jobs or seven years, we are peering into the mists of antiquity, and except in general terms, the information has limited practical value to you.

Asking these questions for each past position helps you find the basic structure of the candidate's career growth and increasing job responsibilities. The salary questions asked for each job ("What did you start at?" "How much were you making when you left?") show you the type of raises this person is likely to be satisfied with and the level of salary increase he or she is in the habit of accepting when making a job change. Sudden jumps in earnings can alert you to potential untruths. For example, when a person with a history of 5% increases suddenly makes a 20% jump, one of two things has happened: Either the individual is fudging the truth or has started to achieve way above prior performance levels—perhaps making a major contribution to an employer. Whatever the case, you will want to know.

However, as just about everyone has fudged on earnings every now and then, you may want to limit the number of black marks you award; it is up to you. Many managers use the exercise just to establish a truthful pattern in the candidate's answers, and when they come across a fudge of this nature prefer simply to let the candidate off the hook with some dignity by saying, "That is such a big increase that perhaps I should have made myself clear that I am just looking for salary, not the value of your benefit package as well."

"What were your three most important responsibilities in that job?"

This is a simple information-gathering question. Jot down the answers and follow up with, *"What special skills or knowledge did you need to perform these duties?"* Combined, these two questions will tell you not only about functional background, but will also give you an insight into the depth of understanding the candidate possesses. If the candidate responds in terms of education, look out especially for any courses or seminars to which a prior employer may have sent the person. This kind of information is useful to you in a couple of ways: First, it tells you that a prior employer felt the candidate to be a good investment of time and money, an endorsement in itself; second, it tells you that such an investment won't have to be made on your budget.

The following questions should be repeated, as your needs dictate, for additional major duties on each specific job within a company and with other employers.

"What decisions or judgment calls did you have to make in these areas?"

The answer to this question defines the individual's level of responsibility, or at least what he or she sees as the extent of that responsibility. For instance, it could be useful to know that a candidate routinely makes decisions alone that in your department would require consultation with a superior. It can be helpful to follow this question up with, *"That's interesting. Tell me how you reached those decisions."* The response will outline the candidate's decision-making approaches for you. You will also listen to find out whether the proper balance is struck between short-term solutions and potential long-term effects of quickly made, and quickly regretted, decisions.

"What achievements are you most proud of in this particular area?"

People are always happy to talk about their achievements, and you are happy to listen for what they can tell you about the individual: Were the achievements something that truly benefited the company and the department, or not? Be especially alert for exaggerated claims, the likes of which we discussed in Chapter Four. This question can often be successfully positioned as the first part of a two-part probe, the second part being, *"Tell me about a problem you experienced in this area, something you found difficult to handle."* This is an example of consciously structuring your negative-balance questions. Whenever you give a candidate the chance to dazzle you with excellence, give yourself the chance to balance the view. Besides, the mettle of a man or woman can often be best judged by how he or she handles adversity.

"What was the most important project you worked on at that job?"

With this question, you are looking for functional fit and will also learn about how the candidate defines important—important to the company, mankind, ego, or whim? Undoubtedly, you are hiring a new staff member to solve problems of some kind, so it would be interesting to discover that your candidate's success with an important project could be brought to bear on some of your upcoming challenges.

"How did you feel about your workload at that company?" and, *"How did you divide your time among your major areas of responsibility?"*

These are both questions that analyze the candidate's time utilization and attitude toward the workload. While you may well decide to probe time management more closely later in the interviewing cycle, these questions will logically fit into the conversational flow at this point and neatly end the question sequence.

Communication

Most jobs today require interaction with others in one form or another. Depending on the level of interaction, your candidate's communication skills and "get-along-with-the-gang" quotient can be vital to his or her ability to do the job. The following sequence of questions will open up this area for your investigation and evaluation.

"How important was communication and interaction with others on this job?"

This is the first question in a sequence that can be coupled with others such as, *"What other titles and departments did you have dealings with?"* and, *"What were the difficulties you encountered there?"* These questions together will establish how the candidate evaluates the importance of communication to the success of the job, and with whom and at what levels the interaction took place. That helps define for you the candidate's level within the corporate hierarchy. The third question in the sequence recognizes the difficulties that arise with interdepartmental communication, and asks the candidate to be equally forthright.

"What was more important on your job, written or oral communication?"

The higher up the professional ladder, the more important written communication becomes. Although most business is initiated orally, almost all meaningful negotiations—both within and without the company—require those convincing arguments to be followed up and enforced in writing. Later in the book, we probe this area very thoroughly in the context of general analytical and problem-solving skills. You may, at your discretion, probe the area here or come back to it later, when you probe all relevant aspects of the candidate's analytical, problem-solving, and communication process.

You may want to request some examples of skillful communication or utilize a little situational interviewing by having the person encapsulate a long report, or tell you which of two reports is the best and why. Nothing's better than seeing communication in action.

"What was the most complex report you ever had to write?"

This and the following questions can also tell you how the written skills could complement or detract from your team. After the description, ask, *"What made this the most difficult report? how did you handle it?"* Follow with, *"Looking back, how would you have improved it, made it easier to understand?" "When have you convinced people verbally of an approach to a task? Give me an example."*

This is a useful question for any position in which verbal skills are integral job requirements. It also gives you an idea of the kinds of things about which the candidate feels strongly.

Common Cause Questions

In the world of industry and commerce, we all have people to whom, and for whom, we are responsible. An individual's attitude toward management, peers, and those lower down the ladder, not only affects the person's ability to do a job, but can also affect the good efforts of others on whom the department and company depend for success.

Ability

"How many levels of management did you interact with?" followed by, *"What was your communication about?"*

The first question tries to discover the levels of exposure the candidate has had working in a multi-level business situation. The second question establishes whether the communication was one-sided (between manager and functionary) or on an equal basis (between colleagues); it will help you avoid being confused by those suffering from the Apollo Syndrome (see Chapter Four). Finish this short initial sequence with two questions that identify the candidate's comfort and intimidation levels: *"What level of management are you most comfortable with?"* and for balance, *"What levels are you most uncomfortable with?"*

Here is another short sequence using the same structure but tailored for a more specific answer.

"Tell me about a time when you had a project that required you to interact with different levels within the company—people above and beneath you. How did you do this?"

After the answer, follow up with, *"Who caused you the most problems in executing your tasks?"* and, *"With whom were you most comfortable?"* The response will always be interesting for two reasons: If hired, the candidate, in dealing with lower levels, will be representing you, and you are naturally concerned that this representation is adequate; and dealing with those over whom the candidate has no authority can require some special skills.

Unpopular Decisions

Any professional job that requires interaction with different people, levels, and departments demands a professional with some diplomatic muscle. Unpopular decisions in such instances are invariably part of the job.

"Have you ever had to make unpopular decisions?"

Find out with the yes/no answer whether the person worked at a level where his or her decisions affected the perceived well-being and comfort of fellow workers. If the answer is applicable, proceed with, *"Tell me about an unpopular decision you had to make,"* and layer it with, *"Whom did it affect? why did the situation arise? how long did it take you to make the decision? how do you feel you handled it?"* Of course, it is a natural time to add at the end, *"What did you learn from this event?"*

All of the above questions, when tailored to your individual circumstances, will address the basics of functional ability. As the interviewer, however, it is unwise to leave this topic without throwing in one catch-all question: *"What other functional, day-to-day activities were you involved with that we haven't discussed?"* Here the interviewee has the opportunity to bring up skills and attributes he or she feels are valuable and that have not surfaced so far in the general flow of conversation. This question can often reveal that small but desirable hidden talent.

Termination: A Bang or a Whimper?

Hiring is usually done in the hope that you will land the perfect employee, someone who will serve faithfully down through the years as *your* star rises in the corporate heavens. Sometimes this dream comes back to haunt us, though, when this valued employee pulls up stakes and moves on. With that in mind, it is better to examine all the candidate's attitudes and reasons for leaving jobs in the past. That knowledge of the past can help us predict, and therefore avoid, unpleasant problems in the future.

"If you went to your boss for a raise, why would you be doing it?"

This may seem like a strange place to start, but closer examination of the reasoning will settle your mind. Anyone initiating an approach for salary or performance review is an individual under some internal pressure from real or perceived lack of recognition and appreciation, and as someone once said, loyalty is a function of appreciation.

Ability

Watch out for answers like, "I deserve it." What you want to hear are citations of solid contributions that demonstrate how the individual has the company's interests at heart. Often, the response will lead the two of you naturally into a discussion about the person's desire to make a job change. If not, the question, *"Have you discussed your desire to leave with your boss?"* is a neat way to guide the conversation around to the immediate results of resignation.

"What will your boss say when you go in to resign?"

This question can be helpful in determining how serious the person is about making a move. All too often, an employed individual uses your job offer as leverage with a current employer, and has no real intent to leave the present situation.

"What was the exact date you left that company?" and, *"What was your title when you left?"* followed by, *"Why did you leave the company?"*

This last question is one of the world's ten most popular—and least effective—interview questions. It became ineffective through overuse, and today almost every interviewee has a pat and acceptable answer in readiness to it. That's okay, because here you use it as the first part of a two-part question. The second part is less common and more likely to get you an honest answer: *"In what ways did your boss contribute to your desire to leave?"* Now, while this question fits very neatly in the procedure of establishing work history and general ability to do a job, it will also shed light on potential manageability and emotional maturity as well.

"Why were you fired?"

There are only two ways to leave a job: You either quit or get terminated. If an interviewee claims that he or she was terminated or layed off, you will—whatever the accompanying explanation—want to verify it when you check references.

"Why have you changed jobs so frequently?"

Unless there are solid reasons for a candidate's job-hopping, you don't want to invest valuable time in a person who is likely to stay with you only a short while. And if you do make the investment, you will at least have your eyes open.

If you discover gaps in the work history, probe the reasons for them and their duration with a question like, *"Why were you out of work for so long/so often?"* More than one manager has confided in me that they sometimes find these reason-for-leaving questions a little awkward. This problem is neatly solved by asking, *"How did you get your last job?"* Answering the question relaxes the candidate after the sensitivity that many people experience when talking about unemployment or job changing. The answer can also profile the candidates' determination, creativity, and analytical approaches to problem-solving, which are three character traits common to many successful professionals.

"Some people feel that spending so much time on one job demonstrates a lack of initiative. How do you feel about that?"

This is a sneaky stress question to throw at the candidate who has marked career stability. The question will come as such a shock that it will give a good reading on fast thinking and poise.

Experience's Big Picture

"What have you learned from jobs you have held?"

This is a wide-open question that provides absolutely no guidance toward a right answer for the interviewee, but can provide you with considerable insight. In the answer, you will be alert for signals that the interviewee has grasped a working knowledge of the workings of the corporate mechanism and the importance of departments functioning as a unit.

"In what ways has your job prepared you to take on greater responsibilities?"

This question is a natural follow-up from the last, or even a suitable alternate. The intent is the same, but the phrasing is a little more direct. You might choose to use this question with less sophisticated interviewees.

What Does the Other Boss Think?

It is frequently advisable to examine worker-manager relationships with a few simple yet valuable questions.

"Whom did you report to?"

This first question of the sequence gives you the name of the individual who will hopefully verify salient facts about the interviewee at a later date. You may choose to follow this with a closed-ended question: *"Will this be someone you will use as a reference?"* It is normal to follow these questions with inquiries about worker-manager relationships: *"What was your boss like?" "How did your boss get the best out of you?"* and, *"What increased responsibilities or promotions were you given on that job?"* are three good questions. The cumulative weight of the answers can tell you how much stock your peer in another company put in the candidate's ability to get the job done.

Hedging Your Bets

It is a common error to assume that every applicant applying for the job is desperate for the privilege of coming to work for you. As a prudent manager, you will be interested in your candidate's motivations for applying, because the right knowledge about the right people will enable you to make appropriate offers to individuals who will actually accept them. No manager enjoys the embarrassment of extending offers that are rejected. It is a poor reflection on selection and judgment skills.

"Why are you interviewing with us?" "Why did you apply for this position?" "What do you know about our company?" "What you do expect out of this job?" "What do you like best about this job?" "What do you like least about this job?" "How will this job help you reach your long-term goals?" "Where else are you applying?" "What reservations do you have about working here?" "What would your references say?"

A selection of these questions as dictated by your personal needs will provide adequate criteria for objectively ruling out some of your short-list of contenders. You will also learn how serious your remaining candidates really are.

Depending on your must-haves and new knowledge of the candidates, you may find some candidates unsuitable in terms of their ability; the rest of the interview might not be of any use to you. You can end the interview for them right now; after all, time is important to you. But it's purely a judgment call on your part. If you are not sure, ask some more questions about areas you still have problems with, or do some situational interviewing. Do anything that will either confirm or deny your suspicions

For the remaining candidates, however, you now have the framework of each person's career and are ready to examine more closely the likelihood of a fit. "Yes, the person seems capable of doing the job," you say to yourself. But is he or she willing to take the rough with the smooth that goes with even the most glamorous of work?

Eight: Willingness

On any day, in any town, in every company and every department, you'll find the clock-watchers. Year in and year out, they extend just enough effort to keep their jobs, but no more. They are the same people who were telling you to slow down and take it easy when you were on the way up. They are the ones long on complaints and short on solutions. They are never happy and never challenged, yet universally endowed with perfect 20/20 hindsight.

Does anybody in your department fit this profile? Not possible? How about the likelihood of your interviewing someone like this? Yes, that is likely. And the problem is that these folks are difficult to spot. Most of the time, they are professionally competent. They *can* do the work, and after all, isn't that where most interviewers stop? They can do the job, and the money is right? Fine, hire 'em! Let's get on with the job. Wrong! Can do but won't do is a bad hire; and don't fool yourself that your magic management touch will shift a career of low gear into stellar overdrive.

The techniques in this chapter will help you probe beneath the veneer of ability and find employees who want to get the job done, to work smoothly with the rest of the department, to meet problems logically and fearlessly, to complete tasks with energy yet with calm. In short, it will help you to complement your team and showcase your management talents.

I'm O.K., You're . . . Well, I'm Not Sure

The first sequence of questions is based around self-esteem, understanding of the job, and what it takes to get it done. You will learn to tell whether the candidate is going to spend time with the critical aspects of the work or whether the unpleasant but necessary work will be avoided with less important tasks.

"What personal qualities do you think are necessary to make a success of this job?"

During your job description development in Chapter Two, you considered the personality traits that would complement the job. Now see how close the candidate comes. You continue the sequence with a follow-up question: *"How many of these qualities do you possess?"* Then you may choose to ask the candidate which of these traits he or she considers to be his or her greatest asset and which traits need further development. Once you have this qualifying information, you can close the loop on this sequence by asking a behavioral question that seeks a specific example. For instance: *"Give me an example from your current job that demonstrates your persistence."*

"How do you feel about your progress to date?"

This will tell you about a person's self-esteem. It will also some times unmask an inflated ego. So, if you ask this question, follow it with a curve ball: *"In hindsight, in what ways could you have improved your progress?"* This second question looks at the candidate's judgment, objectivity, and emotional maturity. Most important to remember with all these self-esteem questions is that you are looking for people who feel good about themselves, because people typically take the same pride in their work as they do in themselves. We are extensions of our professions, after all.

"Do you consider yourself successful?"

This will probably get you only a yes/no answer, which is okay, because you planned it as the first part of a two-part question. Follow up with that wonderful catch-all, *"Why?"* Look for self-motivation, organization, tenacity, and resilience in the answers.

Willingness

"How do you rank among your peers?"

This variation on a theme is designed to probe self-esteem, so expect subjectivity rather than objectivity. On the other hand, the candidate could interpret the question as a request for a factual answer, such as, "I'm number two in the nation." In most instances, it is salespeople who will interpret your question in the latter fashion, in which case you will remember to verify that ranking when checking references. However this particular probe is answered, your follow-up question need not change: *"Have you done the best work you are capable of doing?"* This isn't too difficult for most people to answer, but you must always beware of accidentally hiring a has-been or someone who intends to relax on a reputation for past glories.

"What have you done that you are proud of?"

This is a seemingly innocuous question for the candidate, but the answer will tell you a great deal about his or her vision of work and what areas are seen as important. Are they the same areas you know are important to the work at hand? If there are no accomplishments to be proud of, your candidate is either excessively modest or limited in abilities and willingness, either of which could pose a problem.

"What do you consider your greatest strength?"

This is perhaps the most common of all interviewing questions. (And perhaps the most common answer is, "I'm good with people." If it is not a people job, you have identified a problem: Regardless of other attributes, the gregarious individual will probably never work out well as your night watchman.) This question has been used so frequently along with its partner—*"What do you consider your greatest weakness?"*—that they are both beginning to lose their potency, except when used with entry-level personnel. Listen carefully to the answers you receive to both, and if they sound a little too smooth, it would be a good opportunity to practice your layering techniques with a series of questions examining the what, why, how, where, and when of the candidate's greatest strengths and weaknesses.

"Tell me about a responsibility you have enjoyed."

Here you learn how a person likes to spend time. Is it the area of the job's prime functions, or is it in the area of busy work? You might also follow this question up with, *"And what did you do to meet that responsibility?"*

"Tell me about a project that really got you excited?"

This is yet another way of probing the candidate's motivational focus. It can be tied to follow-ups that probe what happened to the project, how it turned out, what problems arose, how they were handled, and perhaps most important, whether the candidate's obvious enthusiasm led to any oversights or miscalculations.

Getting Along with the Human Race

Willingness to do the job can take many forms, yet ability to get along with the rest of the human race, especially those members who spend their waking hours in your department, is a key element frequently overlooked in the hiring procedure. Here are a series of questions devised to give you insights as to how each candidate works and interacts with others. You will probably be working with the chosen individual for fifty weeks of the year, so find out beforehand who will shorten your life—or career—expectancy with disruptions of your department.

A good time and place for these questions could be after you have taken a walk around the department and perhaps said hello to one or two people. The questions will come naturally then.

"Have you worked with a group like this before?" followed by, *"What was it like?"* or *"How did you handle it?"*

The latter is a little sneaky: It implies that the situation had its problems and needed "handling." As such, the response will reveal emotional maturity and an adult approach to getting along, or else wave a big red flag for you when the person says, "Well, in the beginning, I always find it necessary to tell people exactly how I feel about . . . and . . and . . . "—autocrats like that can sometimes make effective leaders, but they never make pleasant team members.

Willingness

"Did you work much alone in your previous job?"

You need to know whether the person, although part of a team, can function on his or her own. With all the very valuable talk of teamwork going the rounds today, we should nevertheless remember that every team is made up of individuals who need to be self-starting and self-motivating. As a manager, you cannot afford the time to crank-start each member of your team first thing every morning.

"Tell me about a time when you needed to get an understanding of another's situation before you could get your job done. How did you get the understanding, and what problems did you encounter?"

How much does this person consider another's viewpoint? As well as enlightening you about an ability to get on with others, this question also probes the listening profile and analytical skills.

"In working with new people, how do you go about getting an understanding of them?"

Here is another question that covers the twin areas of analytical ability and group interaction. You can look into the crystal ball with this one to those early days on the new job. A follow-up for this is, *"Are you able to predict their behavior based on your reading of them?"* A good question that can generate some interesting responses. As with all answers to your probes, remember that the responses are naturally subjective. Here, you will usually request some specific examples to illustrate the candidate's prior answer.

"What is your role as a group member?"

Many managers find this open-ended question to be valuable in evaluating a person's willingness to get along with others. These same managers follow this opening with, *"Tell me about a specific accomplishment you have achieved as a group member,"* and if necessary, tag on, *"What was your role in this?"* The theory behind the three-part question is that the first reveals intellectual awareness, the second demands a concrete example as proof, and the third completes the loop by requesting the candidate to tie his or her role and contributions into those of the group.

"What kinds of people did you have contact with on your previous jobs?"

This first part of a two-part question identifies the different levels and/or personality types with whom the candidate has been involved. The second question—*"What things did you do differently with each of these different types to get your job done?"*—will tell you about the candidate's ability and range of response in dealing with divergent personality types.

"What type of person do you get along with best?"

This is the first part of a layered, three- or four-part probe. The second is, *"What types of people do you find it difficult to get along with?"* and the third, *"How do you manage to get along with these types?"* You may even want to add, *"Tell me about a difficult situation you had with one of these people, and what happened."* You want to keep the response open, so do not give a lead in your question by adding, "... and how you handled it." That could tell the candidate that you want to hear about a successful solution. It might even be appropriate here to add one of the generic probes: *"What did you learn from this experience?"* Behind this sequence (or any of the other questions, for that matter), is your sensitivity to bringing a disruptive influence into the department. You have no doubt seen the havoc that one disruptive personality can wreak on a constructive work atmosphere.

"What difficulties do you have in tolerating people with different backgrounds and interests from yours?"

This one is somewhat of a trick, as there is the inference that naturally there *are* problems, and encourages the candidate to reveal them. You might find it a useful double-check if not quite satisfied with the sincerity of answers to earlier questions in this chapter.

"When you joined your last company and met the group for the first time, how did you feel? How did you get on with them?"

Past actions can predict future behavior. The answer could well be a picture of what will happen when this person joins your company. Will it be a perfect fit, a case (as the poets say) of "deep calling to deep," or will it presage the start of Armageddon?

Willingness

"Define cooperation."

This is another open-ended, non-directive question that will help build a case concerning the candidate's attitude toward team building and team membership responsibilities.

"How would you define a conducive work atmosphere?"

If the description is diametrically opposed to yours, it could be a sign of trouble. Unfortunately, we spend the majority of our waking hours working, and an unpleasant atmosphere is often a contributing factor to employee turnover. If your employees are smokers and a non-smoker talks about clean air being conducive, both of you could be buying trouble. Continue the sequence with, *"As a member of a department, how do you see your role as team-builder?"* If morale in your department is low for some reason, you might find out whether the candidate is a follower or a leader. Will he or she actively work to improve the atmosphere—to build team spirit—or passively accept the current situation?

"Tell me about an occasion when, in difficult circumstances, you pulled the team together."

This can reveal the person who is willing to take some responsibility for the well-being of the department and the team. However, as the person who initiates such actions is the exception rather than the rule, this is not a question where you should press the candidate for an answer. If a response is not readily forthcoming, move on to the next question.

"Tell me about a time when a team fell apart. Why did it happen? What did you do?"

This is what you want to know: Did the candidate make an effort? where was the finger of blame pointed? at whom? Remember to look for patterns in answers. Beware of a candidate who consistently lays the cause of problems at others' doorsteps—management's in particular. He or she may blame others today; tomorrow, things could change, and the finger of blame might just be pointed at you.

"Have you ever had to build motivation or team spirit with co-workers?"

A positive answer might lead you to add, *"Tell me about the situation,"* and, *"Why had your manager allowed this situation to arise?"*

Analytical Approaches

Analytical abilities, resilience, and certain aspects of emotional maturity can be evaluated when you ask these questions about problems and problem situations.

"Do you deal with complex problems in your job?"

This can itself be an eye-opener when a candidate is obviously unaware of the complexities and subtle nuances of a particular trade or profession. Then proceed with, *"Tell me about a complex problem you had to deal with."* Remember to give the candidate all the time he or she needs to come up with an answer. This area of problem-solving is also ripe for the application of the layering technique.

"What are some of the things you find difficult to do?"

Again, you will want to apply the layering technique here and examine the problem-solving and analytical skills from all angles: *"Why do you find this difficult?" "Where/to whom do you turn for help?" "How do you overcome the problem?" "Where/when does this situation most commonly arise?"*

Decision-Making

"What kind of decisions are most difficult for you?"

Here you will learn about emotional maturity, and in what areas this candidate will spend most time dithering rather than doing. Staying with this theme, continue with, *"Tell me about a time when a quick decision had to be made."* This is another open-ended request focused on the past to provide you with a specific example in response. Weigh the steps the individual took in coming to the decision more than the decision itself. You are not so much interested in the example of a right decision being made (because that's what you are going to get anyway), but rather the analytical process that led up to it. Even imbeciles can make the right decisions once in a while, but usually for all the wrong reasons. Find a man or woman who has a logical approach to problem-solving and decision-making, though, and you have an employee you can rely on.

Organizational Abilities, with Time Management and Energy Levels

Next, we come to the aspects of planning, organization, time management, and energy levels. Those intangibles are difficult to judge, yet vital in hiring someone who is not only *capable* of doing the job but has what it takes to get out there and actually do it. These probes will help you decide whether the candidate is likely to plan projects and budget the available time in a fashion likely to lead to successful completion.

"Tell me about a job or project where you had to gather information from many different sources and then create something with the information."

The answers can be diverse. You can learn about written and oral skills; about creativity, planning, and energy. Overall, though, you will look not so much at the project itself (apart from its applicability to your job) but at the logical and orderly approach the person took to face the challenge successfully.

"How do you organize and plan for major projects?" or, *"Recall for me a major project you worked on. How did you organize and plan for it?"*

A blank look accompanied by a slack jaw bodes ill for your peace of mind. Candidates without a sensible approach to planning and organization will require wet-nursing until you either train them or have to fire them, whichever comes first. Logic and good training should show itself in the answers here. The logical approach to planning and executing major projects includes establishing the project deadline, then working backward to identify key turnaround points in the project. The good planner will explain how he or she builds a milestone schedule with commencement and completion dates for every component part; each stage will include a breakdown of human resource utilization, and thrown in for good measure, there will be an awareness of the need for contingencies.

"Do you set goals for yourself?"

This is a simple closed-ended question that comprises the first part of a three-part sequence. It is followed by, *"Tell me about an important goal you set recently,"* and then, *"What have you done to reach it?"* These questions will tell you about the candidate's priorities, determination, and willingness to stretch for something that's important. And obviously, you will learn about how the candidate is handling current challenges. This particular sequence can be extended with some general probes to verify the person's get-up-and-go quotient. *"Do you always reach your goals?"* could be your next probe. It's hard for the candidate to say no, but watch out for people who *do* always reach their goals. Such claims may once in a while be true, but often signify someone with a poor self-image who sets low goals because he or she is afraid to fail. Every true professional knows that going for the ring and missing it once in a while is part of what makes business and businesspeople successful.

It is especially important to look for negative balance here. Change the pace with, *"Tell me about a time when you failed to reach a goal?"* You want to take a peek at how the individual handles failure, how resilient his or her character make-up is. Will the individual bounce back or wallow in the depths of despond? The ability to achieve success is based on a person's ability to accept the constructive criticism of failure.

"What did you like about your last job?" and, *"What did you dislike about your last job?"*

Here are another pair of common questions that have lost their potency through overuse. If you insert them in a sequence of questions like the current one, however, you can give them new life. Instead of time-worn answers, you will now receive meaningful replies that tell you how a candidate feels about corporate structure and politics, and planning and reporting procedures.

Willingness

"How many projects can you handle at a time?"

This will tell you whether candidates prefer to ride a horse with blinders until one job is finished, or whether they can change mounts in mid-stream, as is sometimes necessary to do in the real world. You can naturally follow this with, *"How many projects do you* like *to handle at one time?"*

"Describe a typical day for me. What problems do you normally experience in getting things done?"

Better to ask this question rather than the commmon, "What is your energy level like?" Otherwise, you will be asking for a reply that would put Bruce Jenner to shame. The description of the day will also tell you something about time management; and of course, energy without efficient use of time ain't a whole lot of good to you.

"Describe a project that required a high amount of energy over an extended period of time."

This question coupled with, *"What did you do to keep your enthusiasm up?"* continues the themes of time management and energy, and adds the dimension of stick-to-itiveness. Business has always been an endurance race, and not everyone has the same degree of stamina. Make sure your team is built with marathon runners. An alternate question is, *"When you've a great deal of work to do that requires extra effort and time, where does your energy come from?"* This examines the same areas and can help you evaluate a candidate's approach to work and problems under pressure. Will she stay calm and get the job done? will he fall apart and waste valuable time confirming an escape route?

"Tell me about a time when an emergency caused you to reschedule your workload/projects."

This can reveal flexibility, willingness to work extra hours when really necessary, and the ability to change course without nervous breakdowns.

"How do you organize yourself for day-to-day activities?"

This one tells you about organization and time management, and can quickly reveal a clock-watcher. This theme can continue with, *"How many hours a week do you find it necessary to work to get your job done?"* Together, they will identify a task-oriented person when you want a goal-oriented one. Be sure to check the hours with references.

"Is it ever necessary to go above and beyond the call of duty to get your job done?"

The answers to this one are always wide open, but beware of the people that portray themselves as martyrs, coming into the office at 3:00 a.m. on Sunday to get the job done. This claim may in fact be true, but such an individual often puts in long hours as a result of poor work habits during the week and is capable of ringing you on the phone at 7:00 a.m. on Sunday just to let you know what a tough world it is.

"How do you plan your day?"

This is a straightforward time management and organization question. Look for individuals who have at least a basic understanding of the essential principles of time management. These include four essential building blocks: The first is the habit of having a set time every day, either first thing in the morning or last thing in the afternoon, to plan the coming day's activities; the second principle is the habit of prioritizing all the planned activities; the third is the steadfast adherence to those priorities as the day's activities are conducted, to ensure that the important, rather than the busy, work gets done; the fourth essential habit is that of reviewing the day's activities for directional changes before planning the next day's schedule. It is known to many as the Plan, Do, Review cycle No one is successful over the long haul without it.

"Tell me about a system of working you have used and what it was like," then, *"What did/didn't you like about it?"* and, *"Tell me about a method you've developed for accomplishing a job. What were its strengths and weaknesses?"*

These three questions all tell about creativity and objectivity. Additionally, you can learn about the determination someone will call on to create new, workable approaches. Listen carefully. You can sometimes pick up a useful trick or two here for yourself, whether or not you hire the person.

Willingness

"Tell me about a time when you came up with a new method or idea. How did you get it approved and implemented?"

You are searching not only for creativity but also for an attention to systems and procedures, and a history of following the chain of command.

"Can you think of a time when another idea or project was rejected. Why was it rejected and what did you do about it?"

This provides good negative balance to the previous question. Watch out for misplaced anger, the finger of blame pointing outward. Look out hopefully for evidence of determination in the face of defeat. Business is about survival, so make sure you hire survivors.

Coolness Under Fire

It is time to look at stress, pressure, and composure under fire a little more closely. If you feel there are never tight deadlines in your department, if everything in your company always goes according to plan, if there is never sickness or employee turnover, if all your people always pull their weight and never run for cover, then you can skip this section. It is intended for those of us who are awake between nine and five every day.

"Think of a crisis situation where things got out of control. Why did it happen and what was your role in the chain of events?"

In a mining disaster, there are always those who will scream against the darkness and those who will light the candles and look for a way out. You probably know your preference.

"What was the most difficult situation you have faced?" "What stress did you feel and how did you react?"

Look for parallels to your situation and remember the above example.

"Tell me about a directive that really challenged you."

After the answer, you can make a secondary probe for originality and drive by asking, *"How was your approach different from that of others?"*

"What do you do when you have a great deal of work to accomplish in a short time-span? How have you reacted?"

With this difficult pressure question, you are looking for emotional maturity or evidence to the contrary: "When in trouble fear or doubt, I run in circles, scream and shout."

"When you have been in difficult and crisis situations, which areas of your professional skills do you vow to work on further?"

This will reveal the candidate's perceived areas of weakness, relative realism, and emotional maturity. You can also tag on these zingers: *"Tell me about self-improvement efforts you are currently making in this area," "Tell me about a task you started but just couldn't seem to get finished,"* and/or, *"I'd be interested to hear of a time when you couldn't complete a task due to lack of support or information."* They will throw light on determination and willingness to accept responsibility for actions.

"Tell me about an occasion when your performance didn't live up to your expectations."

This is a tough one to answer. Give the candidate points for poise and honesty; and be sure to see whether anything was learned from the situation.

"Can you recall a time when you went back to a failed project to give it another shot? Why did you do it and what happened?"

Here's a famous snatch of corporate grafitti that profiles the six stages of a failed project:

1. Enthusiasm
2. Disillusionment
3. Panic
4. Search for the guilty
5. Punishment of the innocent
6. Praise and honor for the nonparticipants.

Willingness

Sad commentary, but often a true course of action for many people, especially those struggling along in the more mature and institutionalized corporations. Someone who has not only experienced association with failed projects but then went back to give it another shot on whatever terms, is certainly worth looking at more closely. But even if you find this rare type, don't become overly enamored before objectively examining motivation; you could end up hiring a modern-day Don Quixote.

Motivational Profile

Motivation and the desire to succeed, coupled with confidence, are important assets for any employee to have. These and other general questions also help to identify willingness.

"What have you done to become more effective in your position?"

Here you learn how important the candidate regards his or her career, and what steps have been taken to forward it.

"How long will it take you to make a contribution?"

For once, the candidate has a wide-open opportunity to sell all the good points. That's okay, as long as you keep your ears open for danger signals such as, "Well, I could get started with overhauling your credit and collection procedures as soon as my coat was off." No matter how competent the individual, a professional knows that it takes a while to understand the fabric of any company and that usually a method exists in the seeming madness of first impressions.

"Why aren't you earning more at your age?"

The composure as well as the substance are important in the answer. This is a stress question, and is used here out of context, precisely to catch the candidate off-balance. Another good stress question might be, *"What can you do for us that someone else cannot do?"* or, *"Why should I hire you?"* There is no way you can expect an objective answer to any of these three. What you will get is a subjective reiteration of the candidate's strong points and desirable character traits, which you can subsequently match against your hiring criteria. You will also get to see how the candidate handles what can be, depending on your intonation, relatively insulting questions.

"How long will you stay with the company?"

This one will often garner the response, "As long as I am challenged." So if you ask it, be prepared to top it with, *"Define challenge for me."* Then sit quietly and don't let the interviewee off the hook until you are supplied with an adequate answer.

"Are you willing to go where the company sends you?" "What are your reservations about living/working here?" and, *"How would working evenings affect you?"* or, *"How would travel affect you?"*

These questions can help define the candidate's willingness to make the commute or the move that your job requires. Please note that these questions should be asked only if they bear direct and important relevance to the job; and if it is necessary to ask the question, you will obviously ask each and every candidate. You must never ask anyone how working late or travel would affect others in his or her family, or how others would feel about him or her engaging in these activities. Such questions are illegal and open you to the liability of a substantial lawsuit; anyway, the candidate's personal relationships are none of your business.

"What books have had the greatest effect on your business life?"

You may be met with a blank stare (which tells you lots) or given a specific answer. Whatever the answer, remember that reading is nearly always done on personal time and therefore demonstrates a commitment to a career. Follow this up with, *"Why did this particular book have the greatest effect on you, and how has it changed you?"* You might go on to see the depth of study by asking for other examples.

"How do you define a successful career?"

The answer to this one can help you find out whether this particular candidate will give your job the effort you'd like. People very rarely do things for others unless the action results in some value to themselves, so you will find a couple of questions about career motivation very helpful. As you are never in the habit of making assumptions, you will ask, *"Is this the type of career you want for yourself?"* You must then consider, based on the answers to these two questions, how long the candidate will be happy in the job.

Now that you know a little more about how to differentiate the willing from the merely able, it is time to find out whether the candidate will be manageable once on board. Remember, gunslingers were always willing and able, but would you want to manage a maverick?

☙ *Nine:* Manageability

"Something should have told me it wouldn't work out," said a manager at one of my recent seminars. "He could do the work and seemed enthusiastic enough, but there was something there I couldn't put my finger on. After the usual honeymoon, though, I began to notice the problem. Things didn't get done, and it was always someone else's fault. Whenever I was away he'd be sick and take time off, or go behind my back to another manager. I tried talking about it to him, but my efforts to solve the problem were always taken as personal affronts. Finally, I had to fire him, but it took me six months to realize the mistake." We went on to spend an hour making sure this manager never again got fooled into hiring an unmanageable employee.

The successful manager builds a three-dimensional picture of the short-list candidates. First, he looks inside, examines the skeleton with questions designed to reveal ability to perform the job's tasks. Then he puts flesh on the bones and gives color and personality with the questions that determine a person's willingness to do the job. Only then does the successful manager get a chance to see the candidate as a whole person. And only by seeing the whole person can the manager decide whether this naked person is going to be manageable.

The questions in this chapter, when customized to your needs, will tell you what each of your short-list of candidates will be like to manage. Your first responsibility as a manager is to get work done through others, so if you cannot manage a person who is able and willing, you can never manage successfully. While these questions will help you understand the behavior and motivations of the interviewee, they cannot help you to get an honest understanding of yourself as a manager; that is up to you. By the same token, very few of us fit that perfect profile of the traditional American business manager, so there is little point in hiring people who can be easily managed by such a creature. We should hire only people who are manageable by *us*, not by some mythical super-manager.

As a manager, you may be the let-'em-alone-type, in which case you shouldn't go hiring candidates whose answers fairly scream that they need constant supervision and encouragement. If, on the other end of the spectrum, you are an autocratic manager, you are unlikely to have a happy relationship with creative self-starters. You know yourself like no one else, and that knowledge must color the suitability of all answers to the questions in this chapter.

"How do you take direction?"

There are two kinds of direction: The kind when you have all the time in the world, and the kind when you don't. If you get a pat answer, follow it with, *"Tell me about a time when your manager was in a rush and didn't have time for the niceties."* Underlying both of these questions is, "How do you take criticism?" *That* is really what you are most interested in, but you don't need to ask it: The previous two questions will give you much more meat.

"What are some of the things about which you and your boss disagreed?"

While you listen to the answer, you will remember not to comment on it, no matter how much you want to defend a fellow manager. You gain no benefit from engaging in discussion about manager/employee relations. Rather, you should listen, absorb, and evaluate: Are the disagreements cited in the answer things that could cause problems for you? For example, if you are the type of manager who does not believe in keeping your employees advised of every corporate decision, you would well have concern with the candidate who complains that a past manager always kept him in the dark, and who found it frustrating to work in a vacuum. No judgment on either part is intended here, yet the dictum "know thyself" should be important here; it is one of the cornerstones of getting work done through others.

These questions are phrased with the current or last job in mind, yet when the area is of interest, there is nothing in the rule books to stop you from repeating the same or similar questions as they relate to earlier employers. Most of the answers to these questions will not be earth-shattering on their own. Rather, the cumulative information and patterns that appear in the answers will give you the key to manageability.

"What are some of the things your boss did that you disliked?"

There is a difference between this and the above question about disagreements—well, there *can* be. One of the two is usually enough, unless the first gets you a really intriguing or disconcerting answer: In that case, offer the second as a further opportunity to expand on the same subject. Of course, you can also keep the candidate talking by adding, *"That's interesting. Tell me more,"* or using a mirror statement. You might even consider using the half-right technique to get at a deeper level of truth (*"So you disliked the way he would talk about other employees behind their backs . . . "*).

"In what areas could your boss have done a better job?"

The answer will tell you how the candidate likes to be managed as much as how he or she *doesn't* like to be managed. It could also reveal some of the criticisms that could be leveled at you in the not too distant future. Would they be justified?

"I would be interested to hear about an occasion when your work or an idea was criticized?"

In this instance, you want to look not at what the criticism was about, but how the candidate took it in and how it is reported to you. Whether the answer is humble or determined to prove the past manager wrong, be especially alert for voice tone and smoldering anger. You can do without people who bear grudges through the ages.

"How well do you feel your boss rated your performance?"
While this one is by nature a subjective question to gauge self-respect and self-image, you will be surprised at how truthful the answers sometimes turn out, especially concerning those areas where the candidate feels underrated. Nevertheless, don't put too much factual store by the answer unless you plan on verifying the performance evaluation.

The Candidate's Management Preferences

Management and manageability probes are not all about looking for the negatives. Looking for what made the candidate's work life pleasant in the past can help you in your evaluation.

"How did your boss get the best out of you?"
Surprisingly, this question is very rarely asked, yet it can provide you with a wealth of information. All candidates, you'll find, will be only too happy to tell you how they like to be managed. Consequently, to know whether you can provide the kind of management under which the person functions best will be of considerable help in your evaluation of all the short-list candidates. On top of this, the answer gives you really tangible advice on how to manage the individual effectively, when he or she does become your chosen and anointed. A neat twist to give to this particular question is to follow it up with, *"How did you get the best out of your boss?"* Again, the answer will show manageability from a different perspective: How are you likely to be supported and/or manipulated by the candidate?

"What do you think of your current boss?"
Another chance for the interviewee to praise or complain. Now, common sense tells even the meanest intelligence that it is unwise to criticize former employers. Even so, ask the question. Some

people just cannot resist the temptation. If you feel the answer is too practiced, or that this question has been answered in other ways before, you might try the following sequence.

"Describe the best manager you ever had," followed by, *"What made him or her stand out?" "How did you interact with this manager?" "How did you react to feedback, instructions and criticism he gave you?"*

Then repeat the sequence in its entirety with this small change: *"Describe the worst manager you ever had."* The responses to these, regularly gathered from all interviewees, can be a very valuable management development tool. They can help you develop your own positive traits, as well as contribute to your effective management of the individual. Both of these questions will tell you a great deal about what constitutes a good work environment for the candidate. Then you can evaluate whether you can or want to provide the needed conducive atmosphere.

You might also look for caricatures of yourself in these descriptions. Once in a while the honest manager has found an unpleasant truth or two. Not to say that you have to hire the person who brings these revelations, but it could help you improve. Do unto others and all that.

"Would you like to have your boss' job?"

Listen closely! It might be *your* job you're talking about. If the answer is yes, ask whether the candidate feels qualified for it and why. It is okay to have someone snapping at your professional heels if it is going to drive you up the ladder. Additionally, you might find this person overqualified or too ambitious for your opening—either bodes ill for potential manageability.

"Tell me about a situation when people were making emotional decisions about your project. What happened and how did you handle it?"

A neat emotional maturity question. If you examine the question in the context of the real world of business, you see that it is really asking, "How did you behave, when for pragmatic reasons and in the best interests of the company, a project of yours was canned or criticized—like a professional or a spoiled brat?"

"Tell me about an occasion when there were objections to your ideas. What did you do to convince management of your point of view?"

This runs along the same theme but from a different angle. And though you've heard it before in Chapter Eight, it remains one of those questions that is difficult to categorize, because any particular answer will reveal different aspects of the individual. In this instance, I place it here for the insight it will give about how far this candidate will push a thought after initial rejection. Pushing it *too* far could present a real manageability problem.

This question seems as though it examines manageability in connection with determination, but it can occasionally reveal some disturbing information. Asking this question myself on one occasion, I gained tremendous insight into the true character of the individual when he replied that he had finally sold an idea to upper management by waiting until his boss was out of town and going above his head. If you get the same answer, the trick is not to fall off your chair in astonishment, but to store this valuable piece of negative information and to go for negative confirmation: You want to establish whether this person will habitually destroy your established systems and procedures.

This may also be a good opportunity for a little situational interviewing. For example, after listening carefully to the answer, you could say, *"I might find it easier to grasp if you could demonstrate that point for me. When I say the solution is too expensive, what would you say?"*

"Have you ever been in a situation where people overrule you or won't let you get a word in edgeways?"

Ask this question when the job requires someone who can defend his or her opinions. If necessary, follow up the affirmative answer with, *"How were you able to get your point across?"* Incidentally, this also tells you how difficult it is going to be to keep his or her mouth shut at important meetings!

"For what have you been most frequently criticized?"

A good, straightforward probe. If the answer seems trite, ask for another area.

Manageability

When the Cat's Away, the Mice Will Play

What the mice do when the cat is away should be of concern to every manager. Often, there are no specifically right or wrong answers to these questions. The answers that match your modus operandi and make you comfortable are the right ones. The others are the red flags.

"How do your work habits change when your boss is absent?" and, *"What problems do you experience when working alone?"*

These will tell you much more than the traditional, "Can you work alone?"

"How do the work habits of others change when the boss is absent?" and, *"Tell me about a time when there was a decision to be made and your boss was absent."*

These questions probe self-reliance and examine how far the candidate perceives the extent of his or her personal authority and responsibility.

"What do you do when there is a decision to be made and no procedure exists?"

This question is a natural follow-up to any of the last four. In the answer, you want to analyze the following: Will the individual come to you? will he or she, in developing an appropriate procedure, stick to the rules, or devise new systems that fit the whim of the moment?

"Give me an example of a time when you were told no. What did you do in response?" or, *"Describe a time you didn't get an immediate yes from someone. What did you find necessary to do?"* or, *"What have you done which required you to ask for something you weren't going to receive right away? How did you react?"* or, *"Tell me about an idea that was rejected. What did you say and do subsequently? What was the outcome?"*

Emotionally immature people seek instant gratification of their desires, immediate acceptance of their ideas, and universal recognition of their talent; as a group, these folks are notorious for their inability to handle even temporary rejection. The answers you receive to this selection of questions will give you a feeling for what to expect from a potential employee when you give negative feedback.

Finding the Loyal Employee

There are people who have loyalty to their company and people who do not. You see this not so much in terms of job-hopping (some of a company's most disloyal employees have been discovered to be lifers), but more regularly in the subtly disruptive influence such people can have over the general happiness and effectiveness of your department. Appreciating the effect this has on your company and career, you realize the importance of keeping these people well away from your team.

"Tell me about an occasion when you felt it necessary to convince your department to change a procedure."

What gets his goat? how strong are her convictions? how valid are they? Follow with, *"How did you go about it, and whose feathers got ruffled?"* You need to know whether the candidate will adhere to systems and procedures in these circumstances and how he or she will go about getting the changes made—like a diplomat or a bull in a china shop?

"If you could have made one constructive suggestion to management, what would it have been?"

The quality of the answer depends on your view of the world. You could interpret, "I don't know," as a response from someone who lacks initiative, intelligence, and motivation. On the other hand, you could interpret, "They should have . . . " as a warning bell on a problem employee. Maintain your objectivity.

"Recall for me a time when those around you were not being as honest or direct as they should have been. What did you do?"

This particular one is very difficult to answer and not sound like Tom Sawyer's milquetoast brother, Cyril. Try to be certain in your own mind of what constitutes an acceptable answer before you ask the question, because it is supposed to probe integrity in a very direct fashion, and should be used sparingly. You may only want to use it if you suspect dishonesty in the department or the company has recently experienced the same. Of course, some industries—retail goods and services, for instance—suffer continually from petty larceny and therefore use such a question quite frequently.

"What is your general impression of your last company?"

This can be followed by, *"Tell me how you moved up through the organization,"* and, *"How did this affect your peers?"* These three questions collectively have a single goal: To tell you about the candidate's prevailing attitudes toward his or her job, peers, and management. These together will spell out whether this person will have a bad or a good attitude once a team member.

"Give me an example of a time when management had to change a plan or approach you were committed to. How did you feel and how did you explain the change to your people?"

This one you will usually ask only when the potential employee will be managing others. It is a complex and revealing question that tells you not only about manageability but leadership, building, and maintenance of the team under pressure.

The Breaking Point

We all have our good days and our bad days, our favorite moments and our pet hates. One of a manager's important roles within the department is to provide a conducive work atmosphere and reduce friction (or at least maintain it at an acceptable level). So, it is helpful to know the flash points of your potential new employees. This is a sensitive area to examine, and nowhere is your tone of voice or the set-up of your questions more important. For instance, it is no good coming right out and asking someone what makes them angry.

"You certainly are a most interesting person. Tell me about yourself."

A little flattery can get you a lot of information at a time like this. Listen to the explanation, but no matter where the conversation wanders (and it is all right to let it wander for a couple of minutes), bring it back to the following three questions about anger. The responses will show you what will make each of your candidates really explode, and that's good for manageability evaluation concerning those positions that require considerable pressure and stress. Ask, *"What are your pet hates?"* layered with, *"Why do you feel this way?"* and, *"What situations can give rise to these?"* Get the idea? Layer more questions as necessary.

"When was the last time you got really angry?"

It is important that whoever you hire is able to control and channel hostilities. If the previous sequence doesn't quite give you all the information you need, you might try this question; and if the cause of the anger doesn't surface in the explanation follow with other probes—*"What caused it?"* for instance. Be sure to find out how the individual reacted to the situation.

If the examples you receive in response to these questions are not job-related and do not shed light on how the individual might respond to stress in a *work* environment, give the candidate more focus with the first question of the last sequence: *"Tell me about the last time you felt anger on the job."*

Oh, the World Owes Me a Living

There are few things more rewarding in a professional's life than getting recognition for a job well done, for effort above and beyond the call of duty. This seems fair and reasonable, so the prudent manager should take the time to see exactly what kinds of rewards and recognition are going to be expected by potential employees in order to keep them happy. As in all the questions in this book, you hope to hear the positive, but must remain constantly alert for the negative.

"Tell me about a time you felt adequately recognized for your contributions."

Manageability

On the downside, you could hear that a champagne brunch will be in order every time a letter gets typed correctly. On the upside, the answer will show emotional maturity and the level of understanding of a specific accomplishment's relative effect on the bottom line. Follow this one with, ***"What kinds of rewards are most satisfying to you?"*** Look for similar danger signals. Most likely you will hear that recognition and encouragement by management is most satisfying; such things are, after all, a validation of a person's career. Layer either of these questions with, ***"How does this affect what you do on the job?"*** or, ***"How does this affect the effort you put into your job?"***

What'd I Do?

In closing this area of manageability, one of the biggest banes of a manager's life is the unexpected resignation. It demoralizes the troops and yourself, puts extra pressure on everybody, and makes you look bad. Time after time, people leave jobs because they did not feel appreciated for their efforts. Often it is the lynchpin of the group, that person on whom you have come to rely, who in fact is *so* reliable that you take him or her for granted until it's too late. You can learn more about how bosses cause resignations unconsciously and thus reduce your turnover by asking, ***"In what ways did your manager contribute to your decision to leave this job?"*** The answers will naturally be subjective, and may once in a while rule out a particular candidate, but understanding the perceptions of yourself and your peers can be invaluable.

Wrapping It Up

Now you know how to smoke out the candidates who are able to do the job, willing to do the necessary work, and able to be managed comfortably by you.

To close the interview, you must recap the areas you've addressed and give the candidate the opportunity to ask for the job or promote his or her candidacy. As we've said before, the interview is a two-way street, and the interviewee needs the chance to get information from you, to make sure that your company can be the place for him or her. After all, you might be trying to hire the best, but the candidate is trying at the same time to hire on with the best. So you should be prepared to answer the candidate's questions clearly and succinctly, and to be generally knowledgeable about the benefits, company goals, etc.

Be sure, however, that you get certain closing questions answered, so that you can increase the odds of your job offers being accepted.

"Are you interested in the job?"
"What interests you most about it?"
"What interests you least about it?"
"How long will it take you to make a contribution?"
"Should you be offered the job, how long will it take you to make a decision?"
"Why should I offer you the job?"
"What can you do for us that someone else cannot do?"
"What special characteristics should I consider about you as a person?"

☙ *Ten:* Backstage Passes

Now it's time to step back from the interview stage. How many interviewers does it take to make a good hire? It depends. Right now, across the country, managers are setting up interviews that involve more than one interviewer. Time and again, you hear that familiar request, "Will you take a look at this candidate for me for a few minutes and tell me what you think?" These second and third opinions are sought because we realize the gravity of hiring personnel, and everyone is reluctant to make the wrong choice. Why? Because getting enough data to make a good decision is perceived as difficult, and no manager likes to make mistakes.

Let's freeze the actors for a moment during a typical "multiple" interview, walk onto the stage among them, and analyze the kind of scripts that have been prepared for use with your job candidates.

To request that colleagues give you merely a second opinion is usually a waste of time. Frequently, the colleague has been given no warning, his or her mind is on other things, you probably forget to furnish a detailed job description and resume, there is no preparation time; and, like most every other manager, he or she will rely on the same trusty six or eight questions that you used to use. You know it's true: Just recall the last time you were interviewed by a series of people for a job. So why do we ask others for a second opinion when they can only confirm what we found out in the first place? do we do it in the blind but forlorn hope that they might stumble across something? or that if they don't turn up something, and the hire turns sour, at least we will not have been alone in our decision? This endless charade is frustrating for everyone involved—even the candidate—yet a very simple solution awaits good management teams, who are prepared to collaborate on their interviewing scripts.

A colleague of mine was able to change this situation in her company. It happened this way: After performing what she was determined would be her last take-a-look-and-tell-me fiasco, she reported the following to the executive vice president: "Nice shoes, nice teeth, poor breath, wouldn't date him." The energetic discussions that followed these pithy observations led to my performing a couple of interviewing seminars for the company and establishing some guidelines that dramatically improved the odds of making good hires. Similar guidelines will help you make better use of your time and your colleagues, while you make better hires and build a better team.

To begin with, give colleagues adequate notice that you need their help to interview, and see how much time will be needed. If you are told 10-15 minutes, tops, look for someone else to help you out—you don't need an unconscious incompetent muddying the waters.

Pick an interviewing team that you can use for all your department's hires. You will work better together and hopefully you can reciprocate. (As an example, Pitney Bowes, among its other excellent hiring practices, insists that a manager from another department be involved in the hiring cycle.) Give each member of your interviewing team your personalized job description and a short briefing. They might find it useful to have a copy of your matching sheet and obviously any written data you might have—resumes, applications, letters of recommendation, etc. Assign each team member specific tasks and go so far as to provide the questions to accomplish your set task. Prepare these and say, "I want certain information from you after the interview, and to help you get it, here are the questions I want you to ask." That way, everyone will cover different ground, and provide you with a three-dimensional view of all your candidates. Your goal is not to get a view of the candidate that merely confirms a hunch, but to get many different photographs from many different angles, through many different lenses. This is the best way to see the candidate whole and make a considered judgment.

Of course, there will be times when you will want your team to repeat certain questions, to see whether you are all getting the same answer. An example of this integrity test would be consistency in employers and employment dates.

Use all available tools—books, prepared lists of questions, etc.—to plan and structure your approach when going for additional opinions. Forget, and the good candidate will be entirely underwhelmed with your professionalism, organization, and troop command.

Often, candidate peers are involved in the interviewing process. Be especially aware of what these future peers are going to say and do if involved in any aspect of the screening procedure. Whereas management traditionally sticks to the same six or eight questions, these guys restrict themselves to three: "What's your greatest weakness?" "How much are you making?" "How much do you want?" All of these are understandably self-serving but potentially harmful to your team-building efforts if you make the hire. Plan what is going to happen and who is going to make it happen beforehand, and appraise those on your staff of their roles and their differing scripts.

The Three-Act Play

How many candidates should you interview for one position? As many as it takes to ensure the long-term success of both your department and your career. And how many interviews should you arrange with one candidate? Again, as many as it takes . . . but let's be realistic. For lower-level employees, one interview with one interviewer is usually sufficient. As your positions move higher up the ladder, the more complex the judgment calls become, and so you may want to arrange two or three interviews. As we are more concerned with the hiring of professionals, who traditionally warrant more careful evaluation, you will probably want to arrange up to three interviews.

Throughout *Hiring the Best*, we have discussed the application of different interviewing styles and questioning techniques to find out whether a candidate is able, willing, and manageable. Now is the time to apply this strategy to an even larger plan. Given this plan, and understanding that the recommended telephone screening is a mandatory part of the procedure, you are unlikely ever to need more than three interviews and interviewers before making a rational and prudent decision. This section addresses how to structure the content of each of these three interviews, to ensure comprehensive and in-depth coverage of the background and potential of every candidate.

The First Interview:

The first interview should deal mainly with facts about ability. Are the functional skills present? can the individual do the job? does the employment history withstand scrutiny? The first interview is a major part of your winnowing process. It should be short; never, ever, make it more than a couple of hours—you can actually accomplish your mission in less than half the time. Those grueling marathon sessions should be restricted to the cream of your short list. Concentrate on ability questions—leave the willing, manageable, and maturity aspects to subsequent meetings. Any situational component would be appropriate here. While I have used examples in the clerical and accounting areas, you can quickly devise a situational dimension for any job. If your company administers any federally approved employment testing, now is the time to do it.

Here, you will want to determine relative strengths and weaknesses, along with the extent of the individual's current responsibilities. If meaningful verbal or written communication is part of the job, now is the time to evaluate and make the necessary decisions. It is also appropriate at this early stage in the proceedings to get all of your personal knock-out questions answered and to discover why the person wants to leave the current job, why you are perceived as a suitable potential employer, and what the candidate will do if you don't offer the job.

The Second Interview:

The second interview deals with facts, judgments, willingness, emotional maturity, and manageability. If you are the group leader, you will have assigned someone the task of gathering the ability information at the first interview and examined the information carefully. Now, you come in yourself at the second level to requalify interesting and sensitive areas, to confirm the ability areas to your satisfaction, and to concentrate yourself on willingness, maturity, and manageability. This is where the probing begins in earnest. You obviously customize the direction of your questions to your unique needs, yet in almost all instances, you will want to address self-esteem, business comprehension, the ability to get along with others, organizational and time management abilities, and degrees of energy and stamina.

Now could be the time for a tour of the facility, as opposed to a walk about the immediate workplace. This could provide opportunities for another situational interviewing play and can additionally provide the impetus for a conversation about how the candidates remain cool under fire, how they bounce back from failure, and how they keep themselves motivated in different situations. If reference checking permission (required under the 1972 Fair Credit Act) has not been obtained, do it now; it will give you permission to check references at the appropriate time. Normally, the permission is included in the application and granted by the candidate's signature, but you should inspect your company's forms to make sure.

The Third Interview:

This final meeting should reprobe sensitive and open areas, and tie up the loose ends. Provide time for any "rubber-stamp" meetings and the opportunity to parade the corporate colors and dazzle the candidate with your eminent desirability. Sometimes, this meeting happens over a luncheon, breakfast, or dinner. (This is a good time to lob a few select and tricky questions specially reserved for the occasion. More of those in Chapter Fourteen.) During the third interview there are some definite musts. Be sure that all of your remaining short-list candidates understand how your company makes money and their would-be role in the process.

Explain what will be expected of the future employee now, when he or she is likely to be most receptive. Outline the department's mission: Your goals and objectives form the umbrella for the future employee's responsibilities. Clear expectations from you at this time will build the candidate's confidence in your leadership, the job, and the company.

The Power Luncheon:

A luncheon or similar quasi-social meeting used as the third interview setting can be a good opportunity to gain additional information that would be difficult to obtain in the more formal office setting. It will also increase your odds of catching the truly seasoned professional with his defenses down. Also, going to lunch has a basic value at the higher levels or with any position where the employee must interact with your client base or the public in similar circumstances. You can learn much of value and surmise the personality of the person while to all appearances only indulging in the simple delights of the board.

Eating in front of others makes people nervous. Throw a question-and-answer dimension in, and you have a stress interview situation created for you in the candidate's head. Even without the questioning, these occasions give you the opportunity to see signs of poor self-discipline, exemplified by over-ordering food and drink. You can observe an inherent insensitivity to others, which could affect team building, in the way your guest behaves toward waiters and buspersons. Aspects of doubtful judgment and emotional immaturity can be detected in the way your guest orders the most expensive and exotic foods on the menu, and what does one think about a person profligate with company money before even reaching the formality of being on the payroll? what is your travel and entertainment budget going to look like? You might also note insecurity and free-floating hostility when your guest starts returning the ice water. The candidate is there primarily to talk and be judged, which is another reason for remembering the 80/20 rule on these occasions. With it firmly in mind, you can eat quite decently as you listen to answers to your questions. (You can always offer your guest a doggy bag at the end, if you don't object to rubbing salt into a wound.)

As far as eating places go, choose a place you know and are known. Book a secluded table—ideally a corner one—and allow your candidate the privilege of sitting with back to the wall. It makes the candidate feel more secure. You want him or her to bare the innermost reaches of the soul, which won't happen if he or she feels on stage or in any way uncomfortable. *In vino veritas*, so offer drinks; you may well have made prior arrangements for your gin and tonics to be light on the gin. To increase privacy and avoid interruptions, order all your food at the beginning of the meal. With these simple matters in mind, you can get down to the interviewing.

Multiple or layered interviews of this nature can take place over a day, a few days, or a few weeks. While there may be enough time to do it in one day, it is rarely practical, except at the lower levels. Such a scenario restricts the ability for your interviewing team to give each other critical leads and feedback on interesting areas to examine further. In addition, a whole-day session is likely to turn that bright young thing into a basket case. Whenever marathon sessions are necessary, give the candidate time to recoup every now and then in a private office, and with a cup of tea or coffee and a telephone. You can use this time to caucus with your team and plan strategy based on the direction the interview is taking.

If you have to drag the hiring process out over an extended period, keep your short list of candidates fully informed. Otherwise that ideal body will be long gone when you are ready to extend an offer.

Perhaps your particular situation requires less than three interviews and interviewers to make a prudent decision on the short-list contenders; it is, however, unlikely that it will require more than three, *if* you engage in effective planning.

Eleven: The Management Hire

All management jobs have this credo: Get work done through others. When the people on your team must also get work done through others, the complexities and critical importance of comprehensive interviewing practices multiply.

To begin with, all management jobs hold certain responsibilities in common, but all management jobs are not alike. Often with management interviews, however, there is a mistaken assumption that all managers do exactly the same work and are for some reason equally competent. This leads to interviewers mistakenly focusing on *technical* rather than *management* competency, with the direst consequences.

While all managers must be able to prove competency in the hiring, firing, training, organization, planning, and people-skill areas, there the similarities cease. The standard interviewing format you might use for nonmanagement ranks must go out the window. Your interview must be custom built for each opening and tailored to the personality of the department as it is today and as you want it to be tomorrow.

Basic Competency

The early questions should deal with determining the size and scope of your candidate's job. While gleaning for you a mass of factual data, these frequently overlooked initial queries will provide some revealing insights into a manager's competency.

"How long have you been in management?"

First things first. Is this a twenty-year veteran from an established company, or a twenty-year-old whizz-bang from a company of two employees? You need to know. With the answer, you must do a little quick math, subtracting the number of years in management from the correct calendar year, and ask a confirmation question: *"So, you've been in management since 1980?"* This information can then be used as a check and balance with the resume data and for subsequent questioning.

"How would you define the job of a manager?"

The idea is to get an understanding of the candidate's viewpoint. The classical definitions don't matter here, just as long as the description matches your needs of the moment. *"How many people do you manage now?"* and, *"What type of positions are you responsible for?"* continue the theme and help determine the size and scope of the individual's department and job.

"Do these people report directly and solely to you, or on a project basis?"

There is a distinct difference. The primary definition of management is the traditional one: The basic duties are hiring, training, supervising, performing salary reviews, and replacing, as necessary, a finite number of individuals. Of course, the scope is often wider, yet all true management jobs include these responsibilities. There are two other possible definitions, however, that the interviewee might be using and which you must differentiate. The first is what is sometimes called project responsibility: For example, you assign three members of your department to work under the guidance of a fourth on a particular project. That fourth person is the supervisor, has project responsibility, but in no way has any fiscal responsibility or the right to hire, fire, or perform salary reviews on fellow employees. If in doubt about which definition the candidate goes by, ask, *"Who performed salary reviews on these people?"* and, *"Who terminated these people?"* They will both help to uncover the supervisor in manager's clothing. The third definition of management is a combination of the first two, embracing traditional management in its accepted definition, with the added complexity of project responsibility on an interdepartmental basis.

Employee Turnover

Time is money, and there are few things more costly to a manager or a company than the time and expense associated with employee turnover. Yet examining a candidate's performance in this area is a subject almost totally ignored in the majority of management interviews. These questions will help you pursue this neglected area.

"What was the turnover in your department over the last two/three years?"

Is the answer above or below what you would expect? Whichever it is, as a competent interviewer you are rarely satisfied with the first snap answer to any of your questions. Instead, you use this question partly to obtain a quantitative answer but, more important, to give the interviewee a focus for the rest of the questions in this sequence.

"What type of turnover was most frequent, terminations or resignations?"

A history of high turnover could be a problem, but at this point you do not have enough information about the reasons—poor interviewing? poor orientation or hiring practices? poor management? poor work conditions? You'll have to ask more questions.

"How many people have you fired?"

This is another straightforward, quantitative question that should be followed by, *"What is the most common cause of termination?"* The response—including the interviewee's tone of voice—can tell you about management style and competency. For example, a manager who explains resignedly about the extreme difficulty in locating competent employees as reason for termination and turnover is really telling you that he or she doesn't know how to interview. (In that case, you will recommend that the interviewee read *Hiring the Best*, then say farewell.) Whatever the answer, follow it with, *"Tell me about the last time you fired someone for this reason. What lead up to it?"* Then, if the information doesn't come out in the story, ask, *"When did you first notice the problem?" "With hindsight, were there any steps you could have taken to rectify the situation?" "At what point did you make the decision to terminate?" "How long from this decision to implementation?"* Each of these questions follows in sequence. With the last one, you may also want to inquire whether the interviewee found it prudent to discuss potential terminations with anyone else before letting the axe fall. More and more, companies are implementing strict termination guidelines these days, to avoid the costly litigation that can result from unfair dismissal cases.

"When were resignations most likely to occur?"

The saying that loyalty is a function of being appreciated has great relevance here. Pay people reasonably, recognize their contributions consistently and in different ways, give them a decent work environment and a positive atmosphere, and resignations will be low indeed. Because a competent manager can achieve many of these requirements with a little effort, responses to your question like "better opportunity elsewhere" and "more money" can sometimes be cop-outs.

If the candidate needs focus for the question, add, *"Within three months, six months, fifteen months, two years?"* An answer in the short-term will give you an indication that this manager's hiring and training capabilities need close examination; an answer in the mid-term could be cause for probing management style and judgments. Remember, however, that people often quit jobs no matter how good the management, so the answer to any single question should never rule a manager in or out. Rather, each answer is another argument in the complex case for or against.

Hiring: The First Step in Team-Building

No sports coach survives long blaming poor performance on the team, and so it is in the business world. When a candidate's abilities in the hiring area are going to reflect on your own hiring abilities, you will want to evaluate this area most carefully. Although you may know how long this person has been in management, and how many people he or she manages and has perhaps fired, you must never take for granted how much interviewing and hiring experience or competency a candidate has under the belt.

"How many people have you hired?"

This could reveal that the interviewee's first and only management job included taking over a fully staffed department with little turnover; consequently, the interviewee will have only slight experience in this critical area. This is occasionally the case in mature and stable companies, where managers invariably inherit a department as a "going concern."

"Have you attended any interviewing seminars or read any books on interviewing?"

This provides an easy way to find out (a) whether the candidate has had any formal training, and (b) whether he or she has made the effort necessary for self-education.

"How do you plan to interview?"

Here, you must watch out for those people who tell you they "like to get to know the person," or who laugh smugly, saying that with all their experience they just "know 'em when they see 'em." These are the Unconscious Incompetents. Follow this with, *"What questions do you ask?"* and then find out what they hope to gain by asking those questions in the first place. If you get treated to "What's your greatest strength/weakness?" and, "Why do you want the job?" push with, *"Tell me what questions you would ask, or techniques you would use, to establish if the person was willing to do the job?"* Then ask the question again as it relates to manageability or ability.

Then, pick an employee type or title that your candidate would be hiring and managing, and ask, *"What are the characteristics most important to the success of a ________?"* At the end of the sequence always be sure to ask whether your candidate checks references. You may also structure other questions around the number and duration of interviews necessary to make good hires, the number of second opinions that would be sought and why, and how a dollar offer is determined and extended.

Agatha Christie's famous detective, Hercule Poirot, was fond of observing the wisdom of asking questions to which he already knew the answer. Here you, too, only ask questions when you know what the answers should be! To take any other approach is to join the I'll-know-'em-when-I-see-'em school of interviewing.

Orientation of a New Employee

The orientation and training of new employees has varying importance to managers in different fields. In all instances, though, the manager is ultimately responsible for getting new employees settled in (orientation) and for getting them up to speed (training).

"What steps do you normally take to get a new employee oriented to the new ways of doing things?" and, *"How important do you feel orientation and training are to the success of a new employee?"*

The great majority of responsible managers will answer that orientation and training are very important. Beware of the ones who tell you otherwise. The manager who lacks these sensitivities is likely to lack team-building and motivational skills as well. These cumulative inadequacies will lead to high employee turnover and all that it implies.

"Have you ever trained other people?"

This is a good opener to get into the area of training capabilities. It should be followed by such questions as, *"What techniques did you use?"* There is a difference between teaching and having an employee actually learn. The answers you hear should reflect this awareness and reveal a manager who is concerned with sharing needed information and skills in a fashion most conducive to enhancing the employee's learning capabilities, rather than talking to hear his or her own lips flap.

"How do you analyze the training needs of your department or of specific individuals?"

Training does not stop once the new employee has settled down, so you might finish the series with this question. It is particularly valuable, because the answer will demonstrate the analytical skills and team-building commitment of your candidate. You may well find the good manager tying the answer into his or her staff performance reviews. One of my clients, for example, recently adapted many of the customized interviewing questions we developed and used them for both performance guidance and appraisal of *existing* management staff.

Staff Communication and Motivation

Modern management philosophy acknowledges that communication and motivation are interrelated skills in the competent manager's arsenal. The inability to communicate appropriately with staff usually leads to staff members retaliating by being unable to interpret directions correctly (you've no doubt seen this happen). Whenever a situation like that arises, motivation leaves by the first train.

"How do you keep you staff aware of information and company activities that might affect it?"

Small companies and growing companies depend largely on verbal communication; written communication comes to the fore with mature companies. If modern management turn-around success stories are to be believed, too much formality leads to communication breakdown and an early symptom of corporate atrophy—something to be avoided. Watch out for the line manager who prefers memoranda to personal contact—it may signify a lack of people skills elsewhere in his or her management style (unless, of course, the memoranda are used to confirm and/or reinforce previous verbal communications).

"Have you ever had an employee suddenly start acting out of character?"

People problems—and we've all encountered them with the staff at one time or another, whether they be psychological or emotional, drugs or alcohol—do intrude upon the workplace. There is an increasing belief that the good manager has a direct responsibility to be on the look-out for such problems, especially when they effect production, morale, and consequently turnover. Appropriate help or acknowledgment of caring can go a distance to increasing loyalty. However, do look for sensitivity and extreme delicacy in the answer. A manager who, without appropriate consultation, oversteps his bounds of authority by getting a drug counselor for an employee, can land your company in a heap of legal trouble.

"Tell me about a program you introduced to improve morale."

This question can be repeated to cover the saving of money, the increasing of efficiency, or the decrease of turnover, tardiness or absenteeism (whatever is most relevant to your situation). Layer them it how, what, where, who, and when questions. There is a specific twofold benefit here. You generate valuable insights into the candidate, and you gain valuable information: Even if you don't hire the individual, you just might come up with a first-rate program that your company could use.

"How do you motivate staff?"

The answer will tell you about the candidate's management philosophy, and even a blank stare can be worth a thousand words. In the same sequence, you might ask, *"Have you ever had to meet tight deadlines?"* then follow the invariably positive response with, *"Tell me about how you motivated your staff when faced with a specific tight deadline."* The relevance of these questions lies in the fact that tight deadlines invariably require extra effort from everyone in the department. Hopefully, your candidate is a good enough manager that he or she can rely on the department's pride in a job well done to pull it together and do whatever it takes to meet that deadline. You are, however, always on the look-out for the manager who uses threats or bribery as a means to meet tight deadlines, because this behavior is symptomatic of other management inadequacies.

Authority and Discipline

An important aspect of management is how authority is wielded and discipline consequently implemented. These questions will also help reveal the candidate's "management personality" and its compatibility with yours.

"What methods have you found successful in setting job objectives for subordinates?"

Management is a continuous coaching and nurturing process. It requires far more than directing the employee to read the proffered job description. Look for a manager who combines both a formal approach to setting objectives and a sensitivity to understand the need for informal coaching.

"Have you ever had to make unpopular decisions?"

You've heard this before, but it has importantant relevance in the context of a manager's world. Setting objectives does not always make the manager a popular person. This is a simple closed-ended question that sets you up for some good layering techniques: *"Tell me about a time . . . " "Why did you feel this was an unpopular decision?"* etc. Most important, to reveal procrastination, ask, *"Having identified that a decision was necessary, how long was it before you took action?"*

"How do you maintain discipline in your department?" and, *"What special problems do you have with the day-to-day management of your staff?"*

These follow naturally from your questions about unpopular decisions. They will shed new light on both disciplinary and management style.

Continue with, *"What are the typical problems and grievances that your staff bring to you?"* and, *"How do you handle them?"* Develop the theme with, *"In working with others, how do you go about getting an understanding of them?"* Remember, an integral part of the manager's job is the ongoing intercourse with other departments, so if necessary, rephrase the question as it relates to other departments, peers, or superiors.

Attitude Toward Management

Your managers are also your employees, and you need to know how *they* react to management. While there are questions elsewhere in this book to help you determine these aspects of an individual's manageability, the following few questions are particularly appropriate in evaluating management candidates.

"Tell me about a time when an emergency/directive from above caused you to reschedule workload/projects. How did you feel?"

This one can tell you about handling pressure and will reveal possible irritants and management conflicts. Teams typically react to situations in the same way as the leader, so check the last answer with, *"Tell me about a time when such a circumstance overrode current activities in your department. How did the staff react?"*

"Tell me about a time when management had to change a plan or approach you were committed to. How did you feel and how did you explain the change to your people?"

You will be interested to see whether the candidate explains the situation to the staff in positive, negative, or defensive terms. It is a weak manager who in such times talks to the staff about "them" and "us," and sides with the employees rather than the company.

Day-to-Day Management Skills

Here is a handful of questions that will help you evaluate how the interviewee is likely to perform on a daily basis with some of those responsibilities essential to every working manager.

"Describe the organization of the department and the responsibilities of each of the staff members."

Here you get good solid data to give you a picture of the candidate at work. It will also shed light on delegation, organization, and planning skills—or lack thereof.

"What method did you use in performing salary reviews?"

You are looking for a logical and consistent approach that shows the ability to track employees' performance through the year against objective, predetermined performance criteria.

"How did you schedule projects, assignments, and vacations?"

Here, you will learn about planning skills and will also see whether your potential manager is reactive ("Well, I just have to cover for them if too many go away at once") or proactive ("I tell all new employees that the department must be adequately staffed at all times and that I require adequate planning notice for vacations").

"What responsibilities do you hold in relation to other departments?"

The answer to this can tell you about committee involvement and how the candidate sees the management role in a larger context. Any interdepartmental coordinating responsibilities can be indicative of room for increased responsibilities.

Fiscal Responsibilities

Four mandatory questions follow—they probe the way the potential manager can handle money.

"Did you hold budgetary responsibility for your department?" "What was it?" and, *"What problems do/did you have staying within the budget?"*

There are many in management who claim that a manager without fiscal responsiblity is nothing more than a charge hand. Whatever your feelings, the level of the interviewee's fiscal responsiblity and ability to manage it effectively are sure benchmarks by which to make a judgment.

"What was your involvement in short-/mid-/long-term planning?"

Budgeting and planning responsibilities go hand in hand, and the answer will indicate whether your candidate is a policy-maker or implementor. This in turn defines another nice difference in management responsibilities. There are numerous people in the ranks of management who implement, but have no input or control over company policy. This question will allow you to see which camp the candidate falls into and consequently whether he or she will be both capable and happy in the job you are looking to fill.

Very Interesting . . .

"How do you quantify the results of your activities as manager?"

The answer should be straightforward—profits, of course—but it will be intriguing to see what the candidate does with it. In the same vein, you might be interested in the response to, *"What would you say are the major qualities a manager's job demands?"* and, *"How would you characterize your management style?"* By this time, you may have formed a slightly different view of his or her qualities and style, so you can make the comparison of views. Be ready with some layering questions to get the candidate to justify his or her claims.

"Tell me about a time when people were making emotional decisions about your projects. What happened and what did you do?"

Emotional maturity and judgment become increasingly important as people enter the ranks of management. This question will let you see right inside the candidate. When all other questions have failed to pierce the interview armor, this will often show you the surprisingly emotional reactions of the candidate to perfectly sound business decisions. It is, after all, rare in business that decisions are ever made on anything but hard fact and profitability potential—very little is left to whim or emotion.

Any manager you hire is, by definition, part of your decision-making team. The care with which you pick such important players should be equally objective and practiced. Leave nothing to whim, nothing to chance.

Twelve: The Sales Hire

With turnover higher in sales than in any other field (20%, according to recent government statistics), hiring the right salesperson is perhaps management's toughest job. The nature of all professional salespeople is to regard the interview as a sales presentation to a prospect, except that this time the product is the one they know best: themselves. They know how to emphasize the good points and minimize or steer clear of the others.

Fortunately, there are approaches to interviewing salespeople that will lower turnover, increase sales, and achieve that most elusive of a sales manager's goals: a competent and tenured sales staff.

You have already been provided with the essential interview structure and with many of the questions. In this chapter, the goal is not to build the perfect sales interview from start to finish. Instead, use the following questions to give you that extra edge in penetrating the competent salesperson's natural defenses. You will discover questions to help you evaluate sales maturity, self-image under stress, and market penetration abilities. You will learn a batch of questions that help in unmasking the truly indomitable salesperson, and that reveal essential telemarketing skills.

Sales Maturity

Success in sales demands a rugged self-reliance and personal maturity. These first few questions focus on the individual's very basic understanding of his or her own needs and also the psychology of the customer and of sales in general.

"Why do people buy a product or service?"

This examines the candidate's understanding of sales psychology. It can be a very tricky question to answer concisely, so look also for professional traits, like the ability to give you a reasonable answer and then end with a question. This gives the control of the conversation temporarily to the interviewee, thereby guiding you away from the troublesome area, and that's a good sales tactic.

"What do you know about our product line?"

This is a good way to follow on from the last question. To a salesperson the interview is a sales presentation, and if there has been no research or preparation for such an important presentation, you will understandably be concerned. Only an incompetent or desperate person would go to an interview without understanding the company product or service line.

"How do you feel about out of town/overnight travel?"

Be careful to explain beforehand the travel requirements, if they are substantial. Listen carefully to the answer. Twenty-five-percent travel—meaning one day in four—will be more palatable to many than three months at a time away from home.

You shouldn't try to find out how the travel will affect the salesperson's family; such questions can often be construed as discriminatory. As overnight travel can put unusual strains on personal time, though, you should suggest that the candidate give these demands careful consideration.

"What do you dislike about most sales?"

This will test quick thinking and creativity, for there are many odious, but necessary, tasks in sales; and the salesperson doesn't want to give you the impression that a "dislike" will preclude his or her doing the necessary work. It's a good question for you, because if the answer is unhesitatingly "prospecting" or "making cold calls," it may well be the last question you have to ask—successful sales are based on making new contacts. You will, at least, certainly have something to talk about.

"What kind of rewards are most satisfying to you?"

Money is always the most important long-term motivator to salespeople, yet ego demands other types of recognition. Find out what these demands will be and whether you are prepared to deliver on them.

"Describe a typical day," "How do you plan your day?" and, *"Why is it important to prioritize?"*

The ego-strength necessary for survival in sales can raise problems of manageability. Therefore, from a management point of view, the candidate's self-discipline and organization need to be examined. You are looking for efficient time-blocking of tasks to maximize the number of sales-calls, and a knowledge of industry patterns. Salespeople must organize their day around the behavior of the industry they serve. For instance, when you deal with the financial community, you keep bankers' hours; when the restaurant business is your field, you keep hospitality hours.

Self-Image Under Stress

Ego-strength and self-image are important components of the over-achiever, a personality type that many believe is particularly suited to sales. Salespeople must not only be able to handle stress, but should find it motivating. Most important, they should emerge from every stressful encounter with their egos firmly intact. This sequence of questions continues to probe these areas while adding to your knowledge base of the candidate's understanding of sales.

"Give me an example of when it was necessary to reach a goal in a short period of time and how you planned to achieve it."

Every salesperson in the world, at some point, has lost business and approached the end of the quota period empty-handed. You are using the question to probe whether or not the candidate can come from behind. Hopefully, what you will get is a "when-the-going-gets-tough" answer, telling you how the salesperson keeps calm, keeps plugging. You will also likely get good question fodder concerning how the emergency arose in the first place—was the candidate perhaps slacking off after a good quarter? did he or she suddenly have to put the heat on to maintain a standard of living?

"How do you keep yourself going when everyone else is having a bad day/is unorganized/is depressed?" and, *"Have you ever worked in an environment where people took advantage when the boss was away? how did you handle it?"*

These will tell you about emotional maturity, self-discipline, and drive. In the sales world, someone has always just lost a sale or a client. It's all part of the territory, and can be a downer. The last thing you need on the team, however, is someone who will be affected by the moods of others. In the responses, look for evidence of determination, a strong sense of self-worth, of someone who is independent and not swayed by the group. As sometimes happens, the candidate will tell you what happens when *he or she* is having a bad day/is unorganized/is depressed. When this happens, you will of course want to probe the cause of the problem. Ask, *"What caused you to feel depressed in the first place?"* and, *"How often does this happen to you?" "What have you done to be more effective in your present position?"*

Here you must look for that extra effort made outside of work hours and beyond company-sponsored programs. Perhaps the candidate has studied the technical side of the product line, or regularly attends seminars, or reads motivational books.

"For what have you been most frequently criticized, and by whom?"

While this is a straightforward manageability question, the odds, in this instance, of getting a straightforward answer from a salesperson are rather slim. Nevertheless, the question doubles very adequately as a way of testing quick thinking and poise so necessary in sales.

"How smart are you compared to your peers?"

This is the first of seven ego-strength questions, asking the candidate for a rating against peers. The others, all finishing with "compared to your peers," follow: *"How articulate are you . . . " "How well-dressed are you . . . " "How witty are you . . . " "How do you rank professionally . . . " "How tenacious are you . . . " "How well do you accept disappointment . . . "* Now, these are all questions expecting subjective responses. By the same token, you cannot possibly be expected to know the candidate's peers. So, don't leave the answers alone, or else all you will get is an impression of whether or not the candidate can talk a good game. Take advantage, rather, of the fact that the candidate willingly takes a position on (for example) why he is more tenacious than his peers. Then, in the second part of the question, ask the candidate to defend the position—just as he or she must do in a tough sales presentation. You begin with, *"I'd be interested to hear of a time when you proved yourself to be more tenacious than your peers."* As you listen to the response, you can well be layering further probes of the event.

"What have been your highest and lowest rankings in your current/last sales force?"

All salespeople know exactly where they rank, so don't let them off with, "I can't remember." If that is the reply, tell them to take their time, then shut up and wait. If you do have to elicit an answer in this way, and you intend to lend some credence to it, be certain to verify it with a reference if possible.

"Share with me an example of surpassing what was expected of you from your employer," or, *"I'd be interested to hear about a specific time when you greatly exceeded the norm."*

It is a chance for a candidate to brag perhaps, but it also gives you the opportunity to see just what this person considers exceptional performance. Of course, if no story is forthcoming, you might be in serious trouble.

Market Penetration

It is always valuable to ask a sequence of questions that reveal how the individual approaches a marketplace, how competent his or her closing abilities are, and how frequently collection problems crop up with the individual's sales. These questions will help.

"What percentage of your sales calls result in full presentations?"

This starter query examines the candidate's ability to get through to the decision-maker. It is unwise to accept the answer as it stands, because it is a very easy statistic to fudge. This may be a suitable opportunity to develop the theme and role-play any difficulties that are typical in your business. You had better find out now that the candidate habitually pitches the receptionist and then retreats, rather than when he or she is destroying your sales projections. A natural follow-up to this is, *"What percentage of your sales calls result in sales?"* Watch for discrepancies: A sales rep, for example, who claims to close one of every two sales presentations and who isn't ranked very near the top of the firm, is either lying or has other performance problems.

"How long does it typically take you from initial contact to close the sale?"

With the answer to this, you can get some help in evaluatıng whether the candidate likes to go for the close or merely jogs along, waiting until the prospect makes a decision.

"I'd be interested to hear about a difficult collection problem you have experienced."

Then follow with, *"In hindsight, how could you have avoided this problem?"* After the answer, ask for another example of the same problem that has occurred since, to see whether the individual learns from mistakes.

"How do you turn an occasional buyer into a regular buyer?" and, *"Have you ever taken over an existing territory/desk?" "What was the volume when you started? what was it when you left?"*

These are all questions that take the focus from the individual sale to the larger picture of the marketplace; you get an idea of how your candidate is likely to accept the challenge. Any market, of course, that has been left as it was found, denotes a lack of skill, effort, and/or knowledge of market penetration and development techniques.

"How large a client base do you need to maintain to keep sales on an even keel?" "Have you ever broken in a new territory/desk for your company?" "How did you like it?" "How did you approach the job?" "How would you go about identifying customers in a new market?" and, *"How do you prefer to go about securing new prospects and clients?"*

These are similar questions taken from a slightly different viewpoint. The responses give you specific information about preferred approaches and can also tell you about the person's willingness to do whatever it takes to get the job done, and the creativity that will be employed in doing so.

"What kind of people do you like to sell to?" and, *"What type of people don't you like to sell to?"* followed by, *"How do you manage to sell to these people?"*

This series will tell you about bias and objectivity and lead you into probing the downside of sales. Follow these with, *"What do you find to be the most boring or repetitive aspects of your work?"* Be sure to ask how the candidate handles these aspects.

"What different types of customer have you called on, and what titles have you sold to in these companies?"

This question is good for raising warning flags and should always be asked early in the process. It is not true that a good salesperson can sell anything. The higher the ticket on the item being sold, the more sophisticated both the buyer and the seller, and the longer the sales process.

"What steps are involved in selling your product?"

Along with excellent written and verbal communication must go good analytical skills. This question will sort out those who happen to be making a decent living in a good marketplace from those who will be able to sell whatever the economic climate.

"How much time do you spend doing paperwork and other non-selling activities?"

Remember to find out what hours of the day these duties are performed, and to match the data with your business' prime selling hours.

"How involved should a company be with its customers?"

You are looking for the insight that maintains an objective distance. The salesperson who gets tied to a client will ride a production crest for a period, but as all clients experience buying cycles that crest and then crash, your best bet is the candidate who combines a hard head with a broad client base.

The Indomitable Salesperson

A successful sales career requires that a salesperson possess large doses of persuasiveness, persistence, and resilience, the three ingredients found in every indomitable salesperson. Here is a sequence of questions to help you evaluate these all-important areas.

"Tell me about your most difficult sale and how you approached it."

The answer will highlight specific areas of interest worth probing further. For example: *"So the sale was difficult because . "* *"Why do you feel that way?"* and, *"With hindsight, what could you have done earlier in the sale to have precluded the problem?"* Good sales managers know that the majority of tough, messy, or failed closes could have been avoided with better initial qualification of the prospect and attention to the details along the way; that's how they got to be sales managers. The question looks for this same kind of analytical ability, with the extra dimension of revealing areas suitable for professional improvement.

"What was the most surprising objection you ever received, and how did you handle it?"

After the candidate's response, create a sequence of questions around the sales objections common in your business. A salesperson's lot is dealing with objections day in and day out, so you want to know how he or she handles the stock in trade. You might begin with, *"What are the three most common objections you run into?"* or, *"What are the very toughest objections you have to meet in your job?"* Then, for all the most interesting responses, ask, *"How do you handle that?"* Situational interviewing techniques are particularly useful in evaluating sales candidates. You can easily simulate real objections by getting the candidate to role-play with you. A good way of doing it is to follow up on the previous question: *"I think I understand but perhaps it would be better if you showed me. If I were the customer and said, 'It's too expensive,' what would you say?"* Short of having the candidate make live sales presentations, situational techniques like this will get you closest to the real performance capabilities. Slip into the format casually for best effect.

"Sell me this pen."

This is such a wonderfully appropriate sales interview question, I'm surprised it isn't asked more frequently. At the root of every successful sale is the salesperson's ability to identify a need and subsequently demonstrate how the product will fill that need. This is commonly known as feature/benefit selling: Here is the feature, and this is what it can do for you. The question tests your candidate's awareness of an essential sales skill and his or her quick thinking. A salesperson is no good if he or she gives up after your first objection. All the above questions will probe how persistent he or she is.

"Tell me about a time when all seemed lost in an important sale. What did you do to weather the crisis?"

Look for a positive and resilient attitude. There is a saying in sales that the sale isn't dead until the client has said no three times. That's the kind of persistence you need to see in a candidate.

"Tell me about your most crushing failure."

Give the candidate all the time necessary to come up with an answer. We have all experienced defeat. You are interested not only in the actual circumstances but also in the spirit with which the candidate handled defeat.

"Give me a specific example of a time you were rejected and how you handled it."

Along with the response, look for that special salesperson who has a strong listening profile and who will draw your attention to the difference between refusal of product and rejection of self.

"Give me an example of a sale that was, for all intents and purposes, lost. How did you turn the situation around and make the sale?"

To keep any interviewee malleable, you must intersperse the tough ones with easier ones. This question is easy for the candidate, but don't you take time to switch off. You just might miss a salesperson who regularly closes sales with deep discounting as the only tool. Look for original thinking and an ability to empathize with the client.

"All of us have failed to meet a quota at one point or another. When you don't meet your goals, how do you handle it?"

This question tests resiliency and can also be a springboard to probe the where, when, how, and why the goal got off track. Very often, the problem is one of prioritization. The next question could be, ***"Why is it important to prioritize?"*** The last in the sequence could be, ***"Tell me about a time when you exhibited persistence but still couldn't reach a carefully planned goal."***

Telemarketing Skills

While not all sales jobs are done exclusively over the telephone, almost all require at least part of the sales process to be completed "on the line." Here is a sequence of questions to help you evaluate effectiveness of your candidates if they have to work over the telephone.

"Have you ever sold anything over the telephone?"

With an affirmative answer, you can then layer: What was sold? how often? for how long?

"What special skills or techniques are necessary to be successful over the telephone?"

To sell on the phone—even to facilitate sales—requires a set of skills separate from face-to-face sales. Because there are no facial expressions or body language to help the salesperson out, he or she must rely on voice inflection, a highly developed listening profile, advanced questioning techniques, and conversation control tricks. Follow up with, ***"Tell me about a time when you called a complete stranger on the phone. How did you initiate a discussion?"*** When telemarketing, it is necessary first of all to reach the decision-making individual, and more and more a company's clerical staff is warned to screen out sales calls. So, along the same tack, ask, ***"When getting through to a sales prospect for the first time on the phone, what roadblocks can you expect the clerical staff to put in your way and how do you handle them?"*** You may even want to role-play one or two of those roadblocks. ***"How do you go about gathering names of new contacts on the telephone?"*** will tell you how an intelligent salesperson can identify new prospects quickly and cost effectively with the telephone.

"What will you do if I don't hire you?"

Here's a zinger at the end of the interview that tests the real mettle of a salesperson. The last person you want to hire is someone who is desperate for any job, to whom you represent a "last chance." While once in a while these candidates will turn into top salespeople, historically the odds are against you. This question will sometimes flush out the loser cowering behind a veneer of success.

Salespeople regard the interview as a sales presentation, and you, unfortunately, are a hot prospect. Most salespeople know that it is easier to sell to a friend—someone who wants to speak with them in the first place—than to a stranger, and that makes your job doubly hard. Be sure to remain objective and methodical in your approaches to interviewing sales personnel, or else you may buy something that you don't really need.

Thirteen: People Futures

Hiring fresh college graduates is like dabbling in futures—a very risky business. And most businesspeople regard hiring entry-level professionals that way: Risky yet necessary, because today's graduate is tomorrow's manager.

That accepted, the correct evaluation of someone with no track record is one of the business world's most sophisticated (and least-addressed) challenges. Good hires should be made on more than grade-point average, and require more than asking the standard questions: You are hiring raw, untested talent.

Potential ability to do the job must be based on academic records and whatever scant work experience exists. The interviewer's true skill emerges, however, in his or her ability to judge the individual's willingness to get on with the task at hand and to complete it. Just as important is the manageability factor, that relatively rare ability among the young to accept guidance and take advice gracefully. Even though the recent graduate must be taught most of the job's necessary skills, there are some he or she should bring to the table: Good listening, verbal, and written skills, initiative, energy, and an analytical approach to problems.

To this end, every trick in the interviewer's lexicon should be called into play, from basic behavioral questions through stress techniques, trick questions, half-right statements, and situational ploys. As each position is different, you will want to include, along with the questions in this chapter, appropriate probes from elsewhere in the book to ensure correct tailoring to your unique needs.

"Are you looking for a temporary or a permanent job?"

This is a good knock-out question to ask early in the procedure, if you start to get a sneaky feeling that the candidate may not be around too long.

"What have you done that shows initiative and willingness to work?"

The answer is valuable because you give candidates the opportunity to tell you some of their perceived strengths. So, by the same token, it is probably wise to balance it with a question about a weakness.

"Which of your school years was most difficult?"

The answer is only important in that it gets the candidate to focus on a tough time. Your data banks fill up when you follow with, *"Why do you feel that was the toughest year?" "What were some of the problems you faced?"* Then, concentrating on them one at a time, ask, *"What caused this to occur?" "What did you do about it?" "If you had to face the problem all over again, would you do things any differently? if so, how?"* The answers begin to tell you how the individual approaches life and its challenges: Head-on, procrastinating, taking responsibility, laying the blame elsewhere, rushing blindly ahead, or planning strategy in a difficult situation. Analyze the answers for pointers toward likes, dislikes, and causes of stress as they would apply to your job.

"Do you think grades should be considered by first employers?"

Whatever the answer is, look for someone who can back up his or her beliefs. The question is not that valuable with a straight-A student, but is very revealing with everyone else, who may feel an understandable amount of guilt that their grades weren't perfect. With those who have perfect grades, you might ask, *"Do you feel you have anything else to learn?"* You thereby gain insight into potential manageability problems.

"So, these are the best grades you are capable of? How do we know you are good enough for our company?" or, *"Your grades aren't all that good. How do I know your capabilities?"*

These questions take the topic of grades and ask candidates to promote themselves from a defensive position. Here, there is obviously a distinct intimidation factor, most suitable when the candidate in mind will have to face intimidation on the job or when it is someone for whom you have high hopes. Your voice inflection is especially important here; these two examples can lose their sting entirely when asked in your best sympathetic voice.

☙ The Future

Having looked at past performance, it is logical to look at the future.

"Do you plan further education?"

The knowledge you gain can indicate a certain degree of dedication to learning and improving professionally. If the courses are relevant to your business, it could be a good sign. But always be aware of that gap between dreaming and doing. This is especially true with recent graduates. They have no knowledge of the extra effort required to work full-time and pursue academic studies. Many are desirous, but few are willing to put out what it takes to accomplish both, so probe to find out how concrete the plans are.

"Can you forget your education and start from scratch?"

This one takes a slightly different tack for relating education to the workplace. The question usually comes as somewhat of a shock to the candidate, so the degree of turmoil or confusion it causes can give you an indication of self-control. Occasionally, it flushes out aggression and a know-it-all-already attitude, which gives you early warning of some tiring times as a manager while you acclimatize this person to the harsh realities of business.

"How did you spend your vacations while at school?"

Perhaps the greatest difficulty about hiring recent graduates is that they are extremely difficult to judge without real-world experience. Those candidates who have some work experience will stand out because you immediately have more in common with them: It demonstrates a basic understanding of the relationship between effort and money. Although college co-op work programs, carefully geared to the chosen profession, are obviously desirable, any work experience is valuable. Even the level of the job is not as important as what and how much the student learned from the experience; and this is where your questions should lead. *"What did you learn from that job?" "Were you ever bossed around? how did it feel?" "What did you like least about the job? why?" "What hours did you work?" "How many days a week did you work?" "What did you dislike most about the routine of regular work?" "Did the job include repetitive tasks?" "How did you feel about doing the same thing time and time again?"* The candidate's answers will tell you about willingness and manageability. In reality, no entry-level jobs are that exciting. Once you scratch the surface, they all carry a fair amount of repetition, so understanding how the young candidate feels about regular hours and repetitive tasks is important.

"What job in our company would you choose if you were free to do so?" "What job in the company do you want to work toward?" and, *"What would you like to be doing five years from now?"*

Each of these probes helps you search for signs of direction, inner strength, ambition, and confidence. The recent graduate may not have much practical experience, but that can be made up for with energy and drive. Regardless of the answer, ask for it to be justified: *"Why that job?" "Tell me what you think a person like that earns?" "Tell me what you think a person like that does on a daily basis for all that money?"* You will find out how much the neophyte really understands about the nuts and bolts of his or her chosen career goal.

"What kind of work interests you most, and why?"

This brings it back to the present and gives you an overall view of the career that the candidate feels would be fulfilling. Once the candidate is finished, follow with, *"What are the disadvantages of your chosen field?"* Complete the sequence with, *"How do you think you will handle that?"*

In addition to the above, include such probes as, *"Why do you want to work here?" "Where else are you applying?" "Do you prefer working with others or alone?" "Define cooperation," "How long will you stay with the company?" "Will you go where the company sends you?" "How long will it take you to make a contribution?" "Why should I hire you?" "Tell me about an event that really challenged you. How was your approach different?" "Tell me about a time when your work or an idea was criticized."*

The hiring decision you make regarding a recent graduate is ultimately a judgment call. You are betting on the future with less than adequate information about the past. As a prudent manager, with the best interests of your company and career at heart, you will reduce the long odds by careful evaluation of each candidate's willingness, ability and potential manageability.

Fourteen: The Clerical Hire

The motor that drives many departments in our companies is the clerical staff. Once merely functionals, the clerical staff is now making a big impact on today's tighter-knit, harder-working companies. The same old typing test and handful of questions in a 15-minute interview are not all you need any more. A bad hire can cause missed deadlines, unmailed reports, shoddy support work, embarrassment. A bad hire can bog you down.

How do you make the right clerical/administrative hiring decision? What questions should you ask? In this brief chapter, you will find some specific questions for clerical candidates. But the general rules concerning ability, willingness, and manageability are applicable here to a greater extent than for managers, salespeople, and other higher-level hires. Much of clerical/administrative work is measured in essential, functional ability. A desire to do the necessary work is critical, especially when the work is not "exciting", and the personal chemistry between boss and support staff can make the difference between a happy and a depressing work atmosphere. The elemental questions concerning ability, willingness, and manageability are found throughout this book and do not need to be repeated here, but certainly you should add some to your list.

The Clerical Career Path

The need for more productivity and more cohesive teamwork is paramount in most companies, but you might be hard-pressed to find an administrative assistant who will burn the midnight oil for you, who will do the extra work you require. One of the reasons for this is that we still consider secretaries, receptionists, and general administrative assistants in their traditional role, as functionaries without the ability to take on increasing responsibility. If no career path exists, why should they come in early and stay late?

If you want to identify and eliminate the candidate who will give only as much as is absolutely required, you should give some credence to the argument for better career paths, and monetary and fringe benefits. The electronic office has increased the number of people responsible for a department's success, so offering the career incentive does actually make sense. Here are some basic but revealing questions that can help you define a candidate's desire for upward mobility:

"Where do you see yourself six months from now?" "Where do you see yourself a year or two from now?" "What job would you like to work toward in our company?" "If you could have any job in our company, which would it be?"

The answers you get will tell you whether the candidate has an eye on the corporate ladder, and that could be the difference between a hard worker and a clock watcher.

If the candidate is seeking a career path, and you have opportunities for growth, you will want to probe the candidate's understanding of what it will take to reach that goal:

"Explain your understanding of the job's responsibilities." "What kind of work interests you the most?" "Tell me what you think a typical day would be like." "What do you think the position earns?" "How will this job help you reach your long-term and career goals?" "How do you define a successful career?"

On the other hand, if you don't have a path to offer, and the candidate has no desire for upward mobility, then you are on common ground and will have to use some of the other questions in this chapter and in the "Clerical Interview Skeleton" (page 251) to gauge willingness.

Reliability

Reliability is a major concern when it comes to hiring clerical staff, and this concern becomes greater as the job responsibilities increase. Poor work habits can have far-reaching repercussions. Some of these questions might help:

"Tell me about a time when, rather than following instructions, you went about a task in your own way. What happened?" "When have you worked on a project of little enough importance that you let it slide?" "Tell me about some occasions when you chose not to finish a particular task. Why did you make this decision?" "What percentage of your time do you spend on personal business at work?" "In what ways do you find work interferes with your personal life?" and, *"Have you ever found it necessary to sacrifice personal plans in favor of your professional responsibilities?"*

These questions are a little pointed, but they can give you a good three-dimensional picture—one that shows the candidate's views both on initiative and on the disregarding of instructions. Do you want an administrative assistant who does what she pleases? Do you want a receptionist who cannot function without direction from his boss?

Flexibility

Clerical and administrative personnel must be able to bend; they must be prepared to adapt to the needs of the moment. Here are some questions that test this willingness:

"Your boss is going on vacation for a month, and although it isn't in your job description to do so, she asks you to work for another manager in her absence. What would you say and do?" "Are you prepared to fill in for someone who has

different, even lower-level, responsibilities?" "Your boss dictates several letters, tells you to sign them, and, as he rushes out the door for a trip, asks you to include a form. You realize after he has left that you don't know what form he meant. What do you do?"

These are excellent situational probes, and in a dynamic office, where situations continually change, it is good to get an idea of how the candidate will react.

Of course, when you hire clerical employees, you will want to examine important elements such as work history, verbal and written communication skills, ability to handle stress, planning and organizational ability, analytical and decision-making skills, and attitude toward teamwork. But hiring support staff can be dependent on the particular "functional" tasks you have on hand. The essential ability to type 60 words per minute—a simple, measurable skill—can have overriding importance in your department. As I said at the beginning of the chapter, a list of general questions is difficult to provide here; and such a list might seem pretty boring and obvious. In the "Clerical Interview Skeleton" on page 251, however, you will find a group of good, ready-made questions to help you probe the essentials of the clerical hire.

Fifteen: Interviewing Within The Law

As I have said throughout this book, the interview is geared to discovering a job candidate's ability, willingness, and manageability. These principles make good sense in the business world. In the world of interview legalities, they make good practice. If they were always followed judiciously, this chapter on legalities (specifically, employment discrimination) would not be needed. Unfortunately, some interviewers still discriminate, and even more are unaware of what makes for a discriminatory interview.

This chapter is meant as a general primer for the interviewer who wants to stay on the up-and-up; it is *not* meant to be a legal guide. To cover every detail of employment law is beyond this book's scope, so if you are ever in doubt about the legal implications of a question, please consult an expert in the law.

Employment Discrimination

The laws, amendments, and court decisions that define and clarify employment discrimination are directed toward the elimination of discrimination in the workplace—toward equal opportunity for all in the land of opportunity. When you make a hire, you may not discriminate on the basis of age, race, national origin, religion, or sex; many states additionally forbid discrimination on the basis of (for instance) physical handicap or sexual preference. By the same token, you may not ask pointed questions at the interview that probe these things.

But what questions are clearly illegal? That is not an easy one to answer. A general measure for above-board questions is this: Is the question necessary to determine the candidate's ability to discharge the responsibilities of the job satisfactorily? In other words, if the question doesn't have anything to do with the job, don't ask it. When your objective is simply to find the most qualified person for the job, you don't need to ask questions unrelated to job performance.

As a general rule, questions about height, weight, age, marital status, religious or political beliefs, dependents, birth control, birthplace, race, and national origin are strictly out of bounds. Sometimes, however, you might find yourself touching on these subjects without knowing it. The following sections will outline some guidelines that I have found useful in discussing the question with concerned interviewers.

National Origin

You should not ask:

- About the candidate's or the candidate's parents' or spouse's nationality, ancestry, lineage, or parentage;
- Whether the candidate's parents or spouse are native-born or naturalized citizens;
- The name of the next of kin;
- The candidate's or the candidate's family's birthplace;
- How the candidate learned a second language.

You can usually ask:

- Whether the candidate is a U.S. citizen or a resident alien with the right to work in the U.S.;

- The various languages he or she speaks (as long as the question is relevant to the job).

Religion and Political Beliefs

The Civil Rights Act of 1964 was amended by the Equal Opportunity Act in 1972, and in it, all matters relating to the examination of religion and political beliefs and affiliations are designated as impermissible.

You should not ask about a candidate's:

- political beliefs or affiliations;

- religious beliefs, affiliations, denomination; his or her parish, synagogue, church, etc.;

- religious holiday observances.

You can usually ask about a candidate's:

- willingness to work on Saturdays or Sundays (if the job so requires).

Even when it comes to character references, you must be circumspect. I have heard of employers who ask for references from a candidate's pastor or religious leader, and that's absolutely discriminatory.

Race

You should not ask questions regarding a candidate's complexion or skin color, or that of the candidate's family. If you still think there's a good reason for asking about race—if you still think that it has anything to do with performance in a job—then you deserve any lawsuit you get.

Sex

The lion's share of sexual discrimination in the interviewing process is directed toward women.

You should not ask about a candidate's:

- change of name, maiden name, or original name;
- current or previous marital status;
- preferred form of address (Miss, Mrs., or Ms.);
- spouse;
- number, names, or ages of children or dependents;
- methods of birth control or reproductive ability.

You can usually ask:

- whether the candidate has ever worked for your company under another name;
- whether any of the candidate's relatives currently work for your company.

◆§ Age

The Age Discrimination Act prohibits discrimination in employment against candidates between 40 and 70. Subsequent state and case laws have effectively widened the range. Ultimately, the only question you should ask concerning age is whether the candidate is 18 years old or not. And if you are ever tempted to discriminate against older workers (as many employers are), ask yourself whether you wouldn't rather hire someone who has already made the big mistakes on somebody else's payroll.

◆§ Convictions

In some states, it is illegal to ask about arrests and/or convictions. Whatever the prohibitions, it is extremely risky to inquire about convictions unless you can prove without a shadow of a doubt that the information has a direct relevance to the job at hand.

◆§ Handicap

The 1973 Rehabilitation Act forbids discrimination on the grounds of physical or mental disability unless there is a direct relationship to satisfactory job performance. This act has opened up a new world for the blind, the wheelchair-bound, the mentally challenged, etc., and has helped them to reveal their potential.

Military History

Most questions concerning military history are illegal, unless the job specifically requires a military background.

You should not ask:

- in what branch of the military the candidate has served;
- what type of discharge he or she received.

You can usually ask:

- whether the candidate has military experience in the Armed Forces of the United States.

Education

You should not ask, "Are you a high-school graduate?" However, you can usually ask the candidate to detail his or her educational history.

As you can see, you must often tread a fine line when it comes to employment discrimination during the interview. The laws in each state differ, and they change all the time. If you are concerned about the bent of some of your interview questions, consult the Equal Opportunity Commission, your state employment organization, your own human resources department, or your attorney.

Sixteen: Hire Consciousness

If you think you have all the answers, you're wrong. You still have to make sure you hire someone from the right universe.

Just as people grow and change during their professional lives, so do companies. As companies go through their different stages, their needs change, and your ability to hire successfully at the higher levels can depend on being able to identify the corporate growth-cycle position of both your company and your candidates.

All companies go through the same five stages of growth. A company at each stage is dramatically different in the weave of its fabric.

Stages One, Two, and Three:

The first three stages are the most readily recognizable: Start-up, growth, and maturity. The first two are self-explanatory. The third is when the company is stable and at the top of its stride. It is characterized in other ways, too: Less of the communication is verbal, more things are written down; more and stricter policies are made; the Human Resources department moves into ascendancy; there is less room for individual creativity; the company is unlikely to be alone in its market; and that market might even be reaching the saturation point. The aggressive investments in marketing that typify growth-cycle companies begin to be replaced by a greater focus on operations. While in earlier stages a company worried more about getting the job done, the mature company, unable to increase sales and profit margins by increasing volume, begins to look more seriously at cost containment as a viable profit generator. Its larger size necessitates more levels of management. It becomes possible for careers to flourish simply by avoiding mistakes, which is frequently possible by avoiding decisions—and as the mature company relies more on committee than on individual initiative, such avoidance becomes easier. Risk-taking changes, too, partly because now any risk is so much greater and partly because of the increasing analysis paralysis practiced by ever-growing numbers of managers and administrators. The once vibrant concern has become a bureaucracy, sluggish with overhead. It behaves like an institution, swelled with self-importance, blind to maladies which it believes to be strengths. The mature company under all these pressures eventually begins to stagnate.

The Fourth Stage:

Here begins the decay stage of the corporate life-cycle: Atrophy. Early signs are an acceptance of the same old profit margins and standards; excuses that the market, the economy, or the numbers of competitors now flooding the field make it impossible for anyone to make a living; and complaints about the lack of competent employees. These are the constant hymns of fourth stage companies. The finger of blame points outward, and no one sees where the other three digits on the hand are pointing.

The Fifth Stage:

There is only one final stage that a company can go through, and one so painful that many refuse to contemplate it. The fifth stage is recognition of atrophy and sustained concerted action to achieve turnaround. Very few companies manage it with any success. Most prefer to let the old tree die gracefully rather than chance the sudden death risked by extensive pruning.

The suitability of a candidate for a position depends on where your company sits, on the corporate life-cycle history of the candidate, and on the personality of that candidate. A person from one phase of the cycle may not be appropriate for a company in another phase. And so, you must prepare for the bad news: ***The most qualified person you can find, alas, may not be the best person for the job.***

Take the example of a public relations director I know of, a man who knows his field inside out, is acknowledged as one of the top people in industry, and who headed the publicity department of one of the country's premier companies. He wanted a new challenge, and a start-up company in the field seemed the answer to his prayers. The company principals were pinching themselves to check that they weren't dreaming: Who would have thought they could land the best in the business? The honeymoon lasted six weeks, and the marriage six months, before the "resignation" was accepted. I was part of the team called in for the post mortem and healing, and saw that the problem was immediately obvious. Our top man was used to managing an established team—the best money would buy—and controling multi-million-dollar budgets. At the new company, his budget was loose change and his staff even smaller. Although no one was better at driving the train once it was out of the station, this particular hot-shot had neither the skills nor real desire to create and stoke the corporate image from a cold start. His skills had passed many years ago—from those of a doer to those of a delegator. The moral is that what you see ain't always what you want to get.

An awareness of the different stages of the corporate lifecycle, with appropriate questions during the interview, could have brought these matters to light and have saved everybody considerable aggravation.

Our example tells us that there could be problems when stars from mature companies join start-ups. These stars have problems when they join growth companies, too, except when the company is approaching maturity and such a person can ease the transition. For fifth-stage turnarounds, you need fresh blood, people who can make decisions and get old hands to stick to them—in short, people who can raise the dead. They come mostly from start-up and growth companies. Yet sometimes start-up, growth, and turnaround experts just do not fit into the mature company. The bureaucracy drives them crazy, and they upset everyone else on the train. Finding someone who has successfully operated in all these phases is rare indeed, as each demands different approaches and skills.

While a senior-level professional may, over the course of years, have practical experience with a number of different corporations—each in different phases of development—it is also common to find people whose sole experience has been entirely with companies in only one phase of growth. For companies in transition from one phase to the next, broad corporate life-cycle experience can be eminently desirable. On the other hand, an individual with a decent track record in companies from a single phase may be assumed to have become indoctrinated by the behavior patterns common for that phase, and might have problems adjusting to your company's own phase.

Now, what does all this mean? It means that in the selection of important positions, you have two major concerns. If your company is approaching transition, you could well benefit from someone grounded in the next phase of the corporate life-cycle. In other instances, you are wise to look for someone who comes from the same phase as your company. This does not mean that you should reject otherwise qualified candidates out of hand. But it does mean that when you identify a life-cycle mismatch, you are obligated to discuss the differences. Perhaps if our example franchise company had identified the differences in this way and discussed them with the candidate, things would have been very different. When hiring never, never assume. The secret is to find out where you are, where the candidate comes from, and then probe the questionable areas.

To this end, you will want to know how long the candidate's company has been in business and about recent and projected growth rates. You need to identify the dollar volume and the number of employees in relation to management ranks—usually the more mature the company is, the greater the number and levels of administrative management deemed necessary to run the operation.

Likewise, the ratio of administrative assistants to management, and whether the employer encourages verbal or written communication, can also indicate how much more formal and closer to bureaucracy that employer is getting, and by inference, how comfortable your candidate is in operating.

❧

Examination of this and other sensitive areas can be done effectively over food and drink and might comprise part of your power luncheon discussions. Here are the questions that will help you avoid hitching yourself to a star from the wrong universe.

"What is the size and role of the personnel department in your present company?"

This is usually the imperative question to ask in this sequence. Personnel, or Human Resources, becomes increasingly powerful in more established companies, so the answer here will give you a general idea about the stage of the corporation. Also, knowing the responsibilities of Human Resources can often lead you into further fruitful discussions about the extent of responsibilities and influence of this department as it affects the day-to-day operations of your candidate's department. These insights, coming on top of your careful evaluation of the candidate's other attributes, can help you picture that person functioning ***in situ***.

"Describe in detail your impression of the responsibilities of this job?"

You have probably asked this question, quite appropriately, earlier in the interviewing cycle, but following our recent discussion, the answer takes on a new relevance. This is where you will catch the misconceptions before they cost either of you time, money, and reputation. The earlier example of the experienced top-dog in the start-up company would perhaps never have occurred if this question had been asked, instead of the answer being taken for granted. This question should be a must in every final interview, so even the smallest misunderstanding is cleared up.

"What interests you least about this job?"

Again, this might have come up at an earlier stage, yet here it takes on a new relevance. It is another reality check on the candidate's perception of the job responsibilities and your needs.

"What kind of people rub you the wrong way?"

An awareness of the corporate life-cycle might make the candidate's people skills worthy of some re-evaluation. For instance, putting a successful bureaucrat among the entrepreneurial types common in start-up companies is to ask everyone to suffer needless frustrations. Follow the subsequent conversation to its natural conclusion.

"With the wisdom of hindsight, what was the least relevant job you have held?"

The response will tell you how clearly the person sees the sum of his or her experience. If the "least relevant" job turns out to be one from, say, a company in a growth stage, and your company is about to enter that stage, then you have gained some valuable information. The answer may also reveal a previously concealed job, which in itself might throw a number of matters out of whack. Alternatively, the answer might fill in that missing space in the jigsaw puzzle that has been nagging you. Of course, to the emotionally mature and truly competent professional, something of value can, in hindsight, be gained from every job.

"Wouldn't you feel happier in another company?" and, *"I'm not sure that you are suitable for the job."*

Earlier in the book, we addressed the judicious use of stress questions such as these. At that point, they were being used exclusively to test poise and quick thinking, and you would employ them as the stress of the job demanded. Here, however, you are using the probes in a far more straightforward manner when you notice a life-cycle and attitudinal misfit between the candidate and your needs. Using the questions in this context, any ensuing conversation will be geared to making the candidate aware of your concerns. You both may be able to put those concerns to rest and go on to experience a mutually beneficial relationship. You also may save each other a professional embarrassment.

Seventeen: Hiring the Best

What is the most difficult type of decision you make on your job? The answer for a manager is simple: Hiring the right person for the right job.

The Hire

What constitutes the right hire? A person who is able and willing to do the work, someone with team spirit and who is manageable, a professional who fits the corporate image and who is personally compatible with your company's place on the corporate evolutionary scale. And of course, an emotionally mature adult with sound and rational judgment will be a necessity in your department.

That is a seemingly tall order and one that has frequently gone by the boards. A recent Robert Half study indicated that American management is three times more likely to hire the last person interviewed than any other candidate. What kind of comment does that make about our analytical and interviewing abilities?

There are several ways in which we can make a prudent final decision and avoid making poor hires that cost time and money, frustration and prestige.

One is the common practice of hiring in the perceived image of yourself or an existing group member. "This is the guy we should hire, he's just like Carole." This is a folly far too common in business. Don't be fooled into hiring to replicate others. Here, just because the candidate reminds us of a good employee, we project a transference of that good employees' skills onto the candidate. Instead, look for balance, strive to add depth to your team; if you already have a few sharpshooters, start looking for artillerymen, pilots, or ballistics experts. A team of young turks should look for maturity and hire people who can share with new generations the practical solutions and know-how that only a lifetime of experience (and mistakes committed on someone else's payroll) can bring.

As there isn't always one perfect choice, compromise and careful evaluation must rule the day. By sifting through the short-list candidates, you will rank the top three contenders. Why three? Because the hiring process is a two-way street, and our first choice may not feel a mutual attraction.

A penetrating interview will have much of the rhythm of a good conversation, and as conversation flows between the past, present, and future, so will your interview questions. The candidate's answers to your past-performance, or behavioral, questions will make you think, "Ah, that's interesting. I wonder what he would do if. . ."

Now, if we accept these past performance questions as offering us the skeleton of the individual, questions relating to the present and future will put flesh on that skeleton's bones by providing new perspectives on the areas of ability, willingness, judgment, and emotional maturity. Then you will see the candidate whole, and only then are you in a position to make that most important determination about manageability.

Will the candidate enhance your department with both skills and a willingness to be part of a team, ready with the personal sacrifices team membership sometimes requires? or will the person's rugged individualism reduce your life expectancy? All these aspects are part and parcel of making a good hire.

There can be little of greater importance than determining the manageability of your top contenders. You can manage some people all of the time, but you can't manage all of the people all of the time; to convince yourself otherwise is to court disaster. Now because managers come in just as many varieties as employees, it really doesn't matter in this context what style of manager you are so long as you know yourself whole and true. When you understand your own strengths and weaknesses, you will recognize far more clearly those types whom you can manage effectively and get the most out of over the long haul, and those whom you should save for another day.

Accept that you will find no such thing as the perfect employee. Look with a clear eye at the jobs you have landed and successfully held over the years. You will find that, yes, you had some of the qualifications, and no, not all of them. You had the desire, some ability and were eager for the chance to stretch. Often, simply matching this profile will give you the best person for the job that you need to fill today.

The goal of Hiring the Best is to give you the tools to make reasoned judgments in the best traditions of prudent management; to avoid putting the wrong person in the wrong job. Your credibility is at stake, and ultimately the stability of your department and company. Disruptions caused by poor hires affect your department's ability to contribute toward the corporate mission. And that can very quickly affect your livelihood. Isn't that where we came in?

Questions. That's how I'll leave you. Always remember that the person asking the questions controls the conversation and guides, in a very important way, his or her own future.

Right?

Special Note on Drug Testing

It is safe to estimate, based on figures from the National Institute on Drug Abuse, that at least one out of every fifty employees uses illicit drugs. Even bearing this in mind, I cannot in good conscience recommend that any company begin a comprehensive drug-testing program, for reasons I will detail in this section.

Our country's ongoing drug problem needs no documenting here. As employers, we are of course concerned about the dangers of drugs in the workplace and their adverse affects on productivity, attendance, morale, and health care costs. For the most part, society seems willing to support private sector efforts to alleviate the problem, yet some significant obstacles remain. In a recent survey by the Employment Management Association, less than half of all workers polled supported drug testing.

The fact is, your organization's reputation as a good place to work can be jeopardized by an ill-conceived testing program. Many managers fail to see the implication of mistrust that can accompany the question, "Are you willing to take a drug test as a condition of employment?" As employers, we must accept that answering that question is likely to be difficult, even if the applicant responding has *never* used drugs. How accurate, after all, are these tests? There is a track record, one that we have an obligation to consult before demanding a yes-or-no response to the query above.

The Message You Send

Here's the translation of that query from the prospective employee's point of view: "Yes; we'd like you to work here, but unfortunately we don't think you can be trusted too far. In fact, we have so little faith in the image you have presented to us that we think you might even be a felon. Consequently, we'd like you to take this drug test." Well? What would *you* say?

I want to note for the sake of background that I speak here not as one with a particular policy agenda to advance, but as a professional in the employment industry who has dealt with this issue first-hand as it affects both employers and employees. Every year I do dozens of employer seminars around the world that address, among other employment questions, the topic of drug testing; every year I talk to hundreds of job-seekers who are confused, angry, or both about how to handle this issue. During one recent twelve-month period, I made over two hundred radio and talk show appearances on job searching techniques; most of them featured call-in segments that focused on drug tests. The vast majority of the calls came from people who had been asked to take the tests and who vehemently objected to them.

These are not drug fiends singing the praises of heroin, cocaine, and angel dust. These are solid citizens who object to the suspension of the presumption of their innocence. They object to the fact that, often, it is the workers on the bottom of the totem pole—the assembly line workers, the secretaries, the receptionists, those who do not have a college education—who are chosen for testing, while the directors and vice presidents somehow slip by. They object to the hypocrisy of ignoring alcohol abuse on the job (and tobacco abuse, for that matter). They object to a system that ignores a solid work record and top-notch references, apparently on the belief that past history is no indicator of whether a worker will wreck valuable equipment, destroy morale, and generally turn the company into a crack den.

They object to all that, and I can't say I blame them. What's more, they have questions to which few employers have ready and sufficient answers. What are the tests really being used for? Will the applicant also be tested for, say, epilepsy, asthma, diabetes—or pregnancy? Who will have access to the information? What guarantees are there that it will remain confidential? What safeguards exist against false positives?

The bottom line is this: When it comes to drug testing, current and potential workers simply do not trust us. (The Center for Organizational Effectiveness estimates found in a recent survey that only 30% of workers feel that employers have their best interests at heart.) Given the current atmosphere that surrounds this question, it is essential to proceed with the utmost caution, tact, and even-handedness, and not simply issue edicts from on high.

What You Should Know about Drug Tests

Sadly, the method of choice when it comes to drug testing on the job is urinalysis, not because it is the most accurate means (it is in fact the least accurate), but because it is the least expensive. This is the state of affairs today; it remains to be seen whether advances in technology will alter the economic choices significantly over the next decade.

Urinalysis testing incorporates up to a five percent inaccuracy rate, according to most manufacturers. Actually, outside of a clinical setting, it is acknowledged that an error rate of perhaps fourteen percent is more credible. For the sake of argument, however, let's take the manufacturers at their word and assume a five percent error. Basically, that means that five percent of the time, the test will wrongly identify someone as a drug abuser, or wrongly give a real drug abuser a clean bill of health. This is a huge chasm of doubt. If you disagree, take the names of your twenty most trusted employees and throw them into a hat. Now pull out one name: what if you had to take as a working assumption that that person had a drug problem?

Remember, we are talking about the potential destruction of careers here: a rate that may seem "acceptable" to you as decision-maker would probably not be "acceptable" if you were the one being asked to spin the roulette wheel . . . and risk your livelihood in so doing.

What causes false positives? There are several factors that come into play, including: the age and/or level of dilution of the testing chemicals; the notoriously short shelf life of urine samples; highly acidic or alkaline samples (often an unintentional by-product of eating spicy foods); temperature fluctuations; unacceptable collection and testing procedures; and, last but not least, reactions to a dizzying array of prescription drugs, non-prescription drugs, or even common foods.

Consider this: Something on the order of ninety percent of all positive drug tests indicate marijuana use. However, the ibuprofen that is used in so many non-aspirin pain relievers can show up as marijuana in the test results!

Here's another example. Assume you are suffering through a bad cold one night and, in order to get a good night's sleep and make it in for work early the next morning, you take one of the popular nighttime cold medicines. The result of your surprise drug test the following morning may brand you as an an amphetamine user! (The same problem may arise with nasal sprays and allergy pills.)

There is a case on record of two Navy doctors who faced serious penalties for abuse of morphine until it was discovered that their test results had in fact been triggered by the poppy seeds on the bagels the doctors bought every day in the commissary.

These are troubling considerations—or should be. There is, however, still something of a cavalier attitude about drug testing among many in management. After all, they seem to be saying, only five (or ten, or fourteen) out of every hundred people stand to have their careers and reputations demolished for no particular reason. What's the problem?

There are some who will claim that my stance on this issue is alarmist, that one would have to eat a ton of poppy seed bagels or consume vast amounts of Nyquil in order to throw the tests off in any significant way. I have two responses to this.

First, it's not true. If the Navy had to admit that it was wrong (which it did) and if the levels of poppy seeds consumed by the two doctors were within the range of "normal dietary use" (which they were, according to the Navy), then there can be little doubt that straight-arrow, upright citizens without the benefit of good legal counsel can be and are being unfairly accused and victimized through false positives.

Second, I have noticed that most of my detractors on this matter are either representatives of pharmaceutical companies or paid consultants for those companies. This is either a sign of blatant self-interest with no concern for the human costs involved, or one of the more remarkable coincidences to come down the pike. I have my doubts about the latter possibility.

Actually, for all the difficulties associated with even the five percent error rate that is unavoidable with urinalysis, it isn't the tests themselves that are the biggest cause for concern. The real danger has to do with human error. Processing the specimens, we must remember, isn't exactly the most riveting or rewarding job life has to offer. As much as we might wish that only top-notch personnel be selected to evaluate those little jars, each representing someone's career, the quality of work is in fact frighteningly poor. The National Institute on Drug Abuse (NIDA) and the Center for Disease Control (CDC) recently completed a joint nine-year study on the accuracy of private sector drug testing laboratories. The result: false positive rates that ran as high as sixty-six percent. That's sixty-six people out of a hundred who could have their reputations and careers unjustly destroyed. And up to one hundred percent of the real abusers were shown to have been erroneously passed. With numbers like that, good intentions and the desire to make a positive statement to the community have to take a back seat. There is, we must acknowledge, a very serious problem with regard to accuracy when it comes to urinalysis results.

If you think it can't possibly get any worse than the statistics I've just cited, you're wrong. With so many flaws in the testing mechanism, it was only a matter of time before the first infuriated employee wondered if there was anything to be gained by talking to a lawyer about all of this. There was. Attorneys I have spoken to look at the fall-out over drug testing as being potentially as lucrative for their profession as the sex and age discrimination suits of the '70s and '80s. If that observation isn't a flashing danger sign, nothing is.

I believe employers should have three major worries about the drug-testing issue as a whole.

- That even with the best intentions in the world, an employer can invite costly lawsuits from disgruntled workers.

- That as the suits get their inevitable share of publicity, the adverse exposure will affect any given company's ability to recruit the caliber and quantity of employees today's increasingly competitive business environment demands.
- That drug testing may make any given company a more likely target for union organization drives. (At present, only union workers have a vocal advocate for their concerns on the ethics of drug testing; the issue is, increasingly, becoming an integral part of major contract negotiations.)

"Damn the Torpedoes!"

Having said my piece on the subject, I should note that, despite all of the problems outlined above, drug testing in the workplace appears to be a trend that is likely to become more, rather than less, common in the foreseeable future. Following are some guidelines for companies instituting testing programs despite the risks and uncertainties I have outlined here.

- *Reduce the odds of a lawsuit* by consulting with your attorney before implementing the program. He or she might tell you, for instance, to test all applicants rather than just the final contenders (many firms do this).
- *Use a reliable test* and do everything you can to protect the rights of current and future employees.
- *Work with a reputable firm that has done work in the field for some time.* By doing so you will increase your chances of conducting the tests with accuracy and sensitivity. Companies that would fall into this category include Syva, Roche Diagnostics, and Marion Labs.

- *Use a back-up test for all positive findings.* It should be a different test to avoid the possibility of the same error repeating itself. The back-up test is likely to be more costly than the initial screen, but it should nevertheless be built into your program's budget.

- *Select a laboratory only after obtaining strong references.* The recommended minimum is three positive recommendations. Be extremely wary of "hard sell" techniques from sales representatives.

- *Visit other employers with drug testing programs.* Take what ideas you can and reject the rest.

- *Establish strict guidelines* for administering and processing the tests, and for protecting the confidentiality of the results. One company I know of gives every job applicant a registration number, a specimen jar, and the telephone number of the laboratory. The applicant gives a specimen to the company, and is informed that the result will be identified only by the number on the jar. After two or three days, the applicant may phone the laboratory and learn the result; at his or her discretion, a second application, which is mandatory for all applicants regardless of the test results, may be made.

- *Provide test-takers with all relevant information* about the foods and medications that can lead to false positives. Ask them to list all medications and suspect foods they may have ingested in recent weeks.

- *Give adequate notice.* You will reduce the impression of coercion if you allow a reasonable lead time. If at all possible, avoid the enforced humiliation of requiring the applicant to give the test in front of a third party.

- *Make sure the right people are administering the test.* Their approach should be personable; they should be able to answer any and every question the test-taker might have. Do everything possible to remove the implication that the test-taker is guilty of something.

Certainly, every employer has the right to maintain a workplace that is free of drug addicts. However, I am not convinced that the percentage of drug abusers now in the work force warrants implementation of programs with the potential negative impact of those now available and affordable. The most valuable capital is human capital; the most powerful resource is people. If we expect our workers to give their all to the work at hand and to the customers we ask them to serve, we must treat them with appropriate respect. Failing to do so will lead them to vote no-confidence in us, and they will cast those votes with their feet.

Interview Skeletons

Here are four interview skeletons. They are sequences of questions, painstakingly selected and positioned, that form the basic structure of interviews for managers, salespeople, recent graduates, and clerical staff. They will be an immense help to you as you prepare for the interviewing cycle.

Of course, one sequence of questions, perfect for every position, does not exist. Each candidate is different, as are each company, interviewer, and position. You will probably find questions in these skeletons that do not meet your particular needs. You may want to add a few of your favorite questions. You may want to replace some questions with others found in *Hiring the Best*. You will have to address the details of your particular position yourself.

And you will have to employ some of the techniques from elsewhere in this book. For example, you will find many questions here that beg for question layering or situational interviewing. You must decide how far you want to take your interview.

I have not included initial stages of the interview—handshakes, exchange of amenities, etc.—nor have I included any questions for the interview's conclusion.

The skeletons are divided into categories:

- Sales: Ability and suitability, willingness, the indomitable salesperson, self image, communication, telemarketing, time management and organization, market penetration, sales maturity, problem solving and decision making, teamwork, and manageability.

- Management: Ability, day-to-day management skills, hiring, employee orientation, communication and motivation, authority and discipline, turnover, fiscal responsibility, and manageability.

- Entry-Level: Education background, work history, willingness and leadership potential, future career, goals and organization, verbal communication, written communication, stress and flexibility, decision making, developmental areas, teamwork, and manageability.

- Clerical: Work history, ability and suitability, willingness, flexibility and stress, written communication, planning and organization, teamwork, and manageability.

Sales Interview Skeleton

Ability, Suitability

Why are you pursuing a career as a professional salesperson?

What are your qualifications?

Of all your work in sales, where have you been more successful, in servicing clients or in developing a new territory?

Would you prefer to sell a big- or a small-ticket item?

When you consider your skills as a professional salesperson, what area concerns you most about your ability to sell?

Interview Skeletons

What aspect of sales do you like most?

What do you find to be the most repetitive tasks of your job?

What bothers you most about sales?

How necessary is it to be creative in your job?

What makes you think you can sell consistently?

Tell me about your training. What have you done to become a better salesperson?

What do you know about our company and its products?

What do you like least about the job description?

What special characteristics should I consider about you as a person?

Willingness
Tell me about a sales project that really got you excited.

What do you consider a good day's sales effort?

Tell me about a time when you exceeded both your quota and your goals.

When the pressure is on, where does your extra energy come from?

How often do you find it necessary to go above and beyond the call of duty?

Do you ever take work home?

Give me an example of your initiative in a challenging situation.

What are some of the things in sales that you find difficult to do?

The Indomitable Salesperson
Tell me about a sale that was, for all intents and purposes, lost. How did you turn the situation around?

What are the three most common objections you face?

What would you say if the customer said, "It's too expensive"?

Tell me about your most difficult sale. How could you have prevented problems from arising?

It is sometimes difficult to get an immediate yes form customers. What do you do in these situations?

When do customers really try your patience?

Tell me about a sale you couldn't close because of lack of information. What did you do?

How do you feel when you get rejected?

Tell me about an important sale that went on the rocks. How did you weather the storm?

How do you react when you miss a sales quota?

Self Image
Do you consider yourself successful?

What do you feel are your personal limitations?

What sales achievement are you most proud of?

What do you consider your greatest strength?

How do you rank among your peers?

Communication
What types of people do you sell to in your current job?

Tell me how you made an "impossible" sale.

Tell me about a time when your timing was good

Tell me about a time when your timing was bad.

What do you do when you can't get a word in edgewise?

Sell me this pen.

How do you get a fix on people in the first few moments of meeting them?

How do you turn things around when the initial impression of you is bad?

Tell me about how your dealt with an angry or frustrated customer.

How often do you prepare sales reports? How detailed are they?

When and where in the sales process have you found silence to be a useful tool?

How do you approach getting an understanding of a customer's needs?

What business or social situations make you feel awkward?

Telemarketing
How much time do you spend on the telephone in your job?

What services or products have you sold over the phone?

What special skills and techniques are required to be successful over the phone?

How do you go about establishing a rapport with a stranger on the phone?

What kind of roadblocks do you expect from clerical staff over the phone? How do you handle them?

How many phone calls do you make in a day?

Time Management, Organization
How much time do you spend doing paperwork and non-selling activities?

How do you organize yourself for day-to-day activities?

Describe a typical day.

Tell me about the planning for an important project.

Tell me about the problems you face in getting all the facets of your job completed on time.

What are the component parts of your job, and how much time do you spend on each?

How many accounts do you like to handle at one time?

Do you set goals that are easy or difficult to reach?

Tell me about some long-term working goals and how you are getting along in achieving them.

Market Penetration
What steps are involved in selling your product?

How long does it typically take from initial contact to close the sale?

What percentage of your sales calls result in full presentation?

What kind of people do you like to sell to?

What kind of people don't you like to sell to?

Have you ever broken in a new territory for an employer?

How do you turn an occasional buyer into a regular buyer?

What was the most important account you have worked on?

Tell me about a difficult collection problem.

What are you most proud of in your ability to develop a marketplace?

Sales Maturity
What would you feel are the major personal characteristics of a successful salesperson?

What have you learned from the different sales jobs you've had?

What aspects of your work do you consider most crucial?

Why do people buy a product or a service?

What kind of rewards are most satisfying to you?

What are some of the things you have found especially motivating over the years?

What do you dislike most about sales?

Problem Solving and Decision Making
What kind of problems do you have to solve as a salesperson?

Do you regard them as complex or overwhelming?

Have you ever made a quick decision that cost you money?

What kinds of decisions are most difficult for you?

What is the biggest mistake you have made in your career?

Do you discuss important decisions with anyone?

Teamwork
Explain your role as a group member of a sales force.

How would you define a conducive work atmosphere?

How do you deal with disagreements with others?

Have you ever had to change your behavior to work successfully with others?

Have you ever been with a sales team that fell apart?

Manageability
How does your boss get the best out of you?

How do you get the best out of your boss?

Describe the best manager you ever had.

Describe the worst manager you ever had.

Tell me about the last time you really got angry about a management decision.

If you could make one constructive suggestion to your current management, what would it be?

How do you take direction? How do you take criticism?

What are some of the things your boss did that you disliked?

What types of decisions are beyond your level of authority at your current job?

If a co-worker came to you with a complaint about the job, how would you react?

Do you feel you are adequately recognized for your contributions?

☙§ Management Interview Skeleton

Ability
How long have you been in management?

How many people do you manage?

What level and types of people do you manage?

How long have you held these management responsibilities?

Do these people report directly and solely to you?

Who hired and fired these people?

How creative do you see a management role to be?

How do you quantify the result of you job?

What do you perceive the responsibilities of this job to be?

How far in advance do you and management typically make specific decisions about directional changes?

Day-to-Day Management Skills
How would you characterize your management style?

Explain the limit of your management responsibilities by explaining the types of decisions that are beyond your authority.

How often do you prepare reports?

With what other departments do you deal?

What responsibilities do you hold in relation to other departments.

How do you schedule projects, assignments, and vacations?

Tell me about a recent crisis.

Hiring
How many people have you hired?

How have you learned to interview?

How do you plan an interview?

What has been your biggest hiring mistake?

Employee Orientation
What steps do you normally take to get a new employee settled in?

How do you analyze the training needs of your department or of specific individuals?

Communication, Motivation
How important to you is communication and interaction with the staff?

What are some of the tasks you typically delegate?

How do you maintain checks and balances on employee performance?

What things cause the most friction in your department?

Do you feel it is your responsibility to adapt to your employees or their responsibility to adapt to you?

With what types of employees do you get along best?

What types of employees cause the most problems for you?

Tell me about a time when morale was low. What did you do about it?

When have you seen proven motivational techniques fail?

Tell me some of the ways you have seen other managers demotivate employees.

Have you ever become involved in an employee's personal problems?

How do you keep the staff aware of company information and activities?

Have you ever faced a situation with a staff member was being less than direct with you about his or her activities?

How do you organize and run department meetings?

Authority, Discipline
How have you been successful in setting objectives for your staff?

Have you ever had to make unpopular decisions?

What are some of the everyday problems you face with your staff?

Have you ever worked with a group that jointly resisted management authority?

What management situation is personally most difficult for you?

What employee behavior gets you angry?

What do you do when a team member breaks corporate policy?

Turnover
How do you handle poor employee performance?

What has been the turnover in your department over the last three years?

How many people have you terminated?

What steps do you make before deciding to terminate?

How have you gone about forecasting manpower needs?

Have you ever experienced problems with company pay scales when trying to attract new employees?

Fiscal Responsibility
Do you hold budgetary responsibility in your department?

What has been the most expensive fiscal mistake of your career?

Manageability
How do you take direction?

How do you take criticism?

What have you been most criticized for as a manager?

What have you and previous managers disagreed about?

What do you do when there is a decision to be made and no procedure exists?

How have past managers gotten the best out of you?

How would you describe the best manager you ever had?

Tell me about the worst manager you ever had.

Tell me about a time when you felt that management had made an emotional rather than logical decision about your work.

When have you been described as inflexible?

How does your job relate to the overall goals of the company?

How often are you involved in making formal presentations or proposals to management or customers?

How do you define the difference between supervision and management?

How do you play the political office game?

What kinds of things bother you most?

If you could make one constructive suggestion to management, what would it be?

Entry-Level Interview Skeleton

Educational Background
Why did you enroll at this university?

How would you describe your academic achievement?

How did you choose your major?

What college subjects have you enjoyed most?

What school year was most difficult, and why?

What changes would you make in your school?

Tell me about your most rewarding college experience.

What are your plans for further education?

What extracurricular activities did you enjoy?

How do you think college contributed to your overall development?

Do you think college grades should be considered by first employers?

How do I know your capabilities?

What have you learned from your mistakes in school?

Work History
How would you describe the ideal job for you?

What kind of work interests you most?

Explain your understanding of this job's responsibilities.

Do you feel you still have anything to learn after all your years of academic study?

Which summer job did you enjoy most?

How many levels of management did you interact with?

What was the job's biggest challenge?

Tell me about a responsibility you have enjoyed.

What has been your least valuable work experience?

How would your references describe you?

Interview Skeletons

Are you looking for a permanent job or do you plan to return to school?

Willingness, Leadership Potential
If you were hiring a graduate for this position, what would you be looking for?

What have you done that shows initiative and willingness to work?

What would you look for in potential leaders for this organization?

What experience have you had in leadership positions?

As a leader, have your decisions ever been unpopular?

When the pressure of work is high, where does your energy come from?

Tell me about a time when unexpected events demanded that you reschedule your time.

Future Career
Why are you interviewing with us?

What do you know about our company?

What do you expect out of this job?

What do you like best about this job?

What do you like least?

How will this job help you reach your long-term personal and career goals?

What is more important at the start of your career, money or the job?

What do you feel are the disadvantages of this field?

Where do you think you could make the biggest contribution to this organization?

What do you see yourself doing five years from now?

How long would you anticipate staying with the company?

How do you define a successful career?

What can you do for us that someone else can't?

What special characteristics should I consider about you?

Goals, Organization
What are your long-range goals?

How do you plan your day, your week?

How do you determine your priorities?

An overwhelming, time-sensitive task has just been assigned to you. How do you plan strategy for meeting your deadline?

What happens when two priorities compete for your time?

When short-term goals clash with long-term ones, which takes priority and why?

Verbal Communication
Getting the job done involves gathering information and input from others. How do you do this?

What is the toughest communication problem you have faced?

Tell me how you have verbally convinced someone of an approach or an idea

Tell me about a time you have compromised successfully.

In what situations are you inflexible?

How do you overcome objections to your ideas?

Written Communication
When have your verbal communications been important enough to follow up in writing?

Are there situations better suited to written communication?

What is the most difficult paper you have written?

Stress, Flexibility
Tell me about a time when someone lost his or her temper at you in a business environment.

Have you ever worked in a place where it seemed to be one crisis after another?

What makes you feel tense or nervous?

What is the most frustrating work-related experience you have faced?

What do you do when you are being pressed for a decision?

Decision Making
How will you evaluate the company for which you hope to work?

What makes you think you have what it takes to be successful in this business?

Do you take an intuitive or a logical approach to solving problems?

What kinds of decisions are toughest for you?

Developmental Areas
What do you see as some of your most pressing developmental needs?

What have you been involved with that you now regret?

What is the biggest single mistake you have made?

What have the disappointments of life taught you?

Tell me about something you started but couldn't finish.

Teamwork
Define cooperation.

What is the difference between a friend and a colleague?

Can you think of a time when you have successfully motivated friends or colleagues to achieve a difficult goal?

How will you establish a working relationship with the employees in this company?

How would you work with the various different opinions in a team in order to reach a goal?

Define a good work atmosphere.

What are some of the common friction areas you watch for when working with others?

Manageability
What qualities should a successful manager possess?

What do you feel should be the relationship between the manager and the staff?

How have past managers gotten the best out of you?

Describe the toughest manager you ever had.

How do you take direction?

How do you take criticism?

Tell me about an occasion when school or employer policies have been unfair to you.

For what have you been most frequently criticized?

Clerical Interview Skeleton

Work History
Describe a typical work day.

What skills can you bring to this position, other than the ones required in the job description?

What accomplishments are you most proud of?

What aspects of your job give you most enjoyment?

What aspects of your job cause you the most problems?

Ability, Suitability
What would you change about your current job?

How do you handle repetitive tasks?

What are you looking for in your next job?

What are the personal qualities this job demands?

What aspects of your job do you consider the most crucial?

How would you describe yourself in terms of your work?

Tell me about your role in a crisis situation.

Have you ever worked for more than one manager?

How does your job relate to the overall success or your department and your company?

Tell me about a time when the boss was absent and you had to make a decision.

What special responsibilities or assignments have you been given?

Tell me about an occasion when you chose, for whatever reason, not to finish a particular task.

Have you ever found it necessary to sacrifice personal plans in favor of your professional responsibilities?

Are you prepared to perform duties that may not be part of your routine?

Describe what you think a typical day would be like on this job.

Tell me about a time when your performance did not live up to your expectations.

Where do you see yourself six months from now?

What kind of work interests you most?

If you could have any job in this company, what would it be?

How would that job help you reach your long-term personal and career goals?

How do you define a successful career?

Willingness
Do you ever find it necessary to go beyond the call of duty to get a job done?

What role do you play in ensuring a smooth working environment when your boss is away?

What have you done to become more effective in your career?

If you went to your boss for a raise, why would you be doing it?

Interview Skeletons

Flexibility, Stress
How many levels of management do you deal with?

What type of people do you get along with best?

How do you get along with people whom you don't like?

How necessary is it to be creative in your job?

Describe the toughest situation you have ever faced.

How many projects can you handle at a time?

How do you prioritize your projects?

When have you rescheduled your time to accommodate an unexpected workload?

Have you ever been affected by communication problems between two managers?

Have you ever dealt with the general public?

Do you handle personal matters for your boss?

When was the last time something or someone got you really upset at work?

Tell me about a time when you put your foot in your mouth.

The receptionist has gone home sick. Are you prepared to fill in for her, even though the job is beneath your level of responsibilities?

Written Communication
Tell me about the kinds of communication you type at work.

Do you ever compose letters for others?

How do you set up a letter? an invoice?

What was the most complex document you ever produced?

What forms or documents have you developed for your department?

Planning, Organization
Describe your method for keeping track of important matters.

How do you plan your day?

How would you plan for a major project?

Do you set goals for yourself?

Tell me about a time when, despite careful planning, things got out of hand.

Teamwork
Have you ever worked with a group like this before?

How do you establish a working relationship with new people?

Tell me how you see your responsibilities as a group member.

What kind of people do you like to work with?

What kind of people do you dislike to work with?

What do you do when you have to work with these people?

Have you ever had to stifle your normal behavior to get along with someone?

How do you feel about people who don't like their jobs?

How do you define a conducive work atmosphere?

Manageability
How does your boss get the best out of you?

How do you get the best out of your boss?

What do you think of your current boss?

Describe the best manager you ever had.

Describe the worst manager you ever had.

What made them stand out?

How do you react to criticism?

How do you take direction?

Describe the toughest manager you ever worked for.

Tell me about the kind of rewards that make you feel adequately recognized for your contributions.

How do your work habits change when your boss is out of the office?

How could your boss do a better job?

In what ways has your boss contributed to your reason for leaving your job?

About the Author:

Martin John Yate, an internationally published author and syndicated feature writer, is also a noted employment/management lecturer. Born and educated in England, he moved to the U.S. and served as Director of Personnel for Bell Industries Computer Memory Division and then as Director of Training for the Dunhill Personnel System, one of the largest personnel services organizations in the country.

Currently, he is a special training consultant to some of the leading companies in the employment services industry and the corporate world, and conducts seminars nationally on all aspects of the hiring and interviewing process. He lives on Long Island.